throwing up Fortifications an[illegible] ter but that Paredes has left [illegible] of Nine thousand more to reinforce [illegible] the latest news says that he has been obliged to return to the City of Mexico on account of some ruption there. But a few months more will determine what we have to do, and I will be careful to keep my dear Julia advised of what the army in this quarter is about. Fred. has not arrived here yet but I am looking for him daily. His commission arrived some time ago and also a letter from St. Louis for him. I have them both in my possession and wrote to him to hasten on. His Regt. (the 5th Infantry) is already in Camargo. A few months more of fatigue and privation, I am much in hopes, will bring our difficulties to such a crisis that I will be able to see you again Julia, and then if my wishes prevail, we would never part again as merely engaged but as,—you know what I would say. No doubt a hard March awaits us between Camargo and Monterey. The distance is over two hundred miles and as I have understood, a great part of it without water. But a person cannot expect to make a Campaign without meeting with some privations. Fred. and me will probably be near each other during the time and between us I am in hopes that I will hear from my dear Julia very only but write oftener to me than to Fred.— Since we have been in Mata

MY DEAREST JULIA

My Dearest Julia

THE WARTIME LETTERS OF ULYSSES S. GRANT TO HIS WIFE

☆ ☆ ☆

WITH AN INTRODUCTION BY

RON CHERNOW

LIBRARY OF AMERICA

Special Publication

MY DEAREST JULIA

Published in the United States by Library of America.
www.loa.org

All texts published by arrangement with the Ulysses S. Grant Association.

Frontispiece photograph of Julia Dent Grant, c. 1855–61.
Courtesy of the National First Ladies' Library.

Distributed to the trade in the United States by Penguin Random House Inc. and in Canada by Penguin Random House Canada Ltd.

Library of Congress Control Number: 2018935011
ISBN 978-1-59853-589-1

3 5 7 9 10 8 6 4 2

Manufactured in the United States of America

CONTENTS

☆ ☆ ☆

INTRODUCTION

by Ron Chernow

WHEN ULYSSES S. GRANT wrote his *Personal Memoirs*—certainly the most brilliant military memoirs in American letters—during the final year of his life, those who knew him most intimately were least surprised by their exceptional literary merit. "In their line, there is no higher literature than those modest, simple 'memoirs,'" insisted Mark Twain (Samuel Clemens), who served as their publisher. Grant had long prided himself on his writing. During the Civil War, he had composed his own military orders, sometimes dashing off several dozen at a rapid clip in a terse, letter-perfect style. And as president he had drafted his addresses and messages in the days before professional speechwriters became fixtures in the White House.

So durable has been the stereotype of Grant as a stoic and laconic soul that most readers will be struck by the tender tone of the letters he wrote to his wife, Julia, eighty-five of which have now been collected in this fine volume by the Library of America editors. However spare in style, they candidly portray Grant's emotional state, showing his remarkable evolution from an insecure young soldier to a capable, self-confident general. A man so reserved in public needed a private outlet for his feelings, and his correspondence with Julia was the ideal repository for these confessions.

After graduating from West Point in 1843, Grant was posted as a second lieutenant to Jefferson Barracks near St. Louis, where he met Julia Dent, sister of a West Point roommate. It was the sort of classic mismatch that, through love's strange alchemy, sometimes yields marital bliss. Grant had grown up in several small rural towns in southwest Ohio, the son of strait-laced Methodist parents, who frowned on dancing, drinking, and card-playing. Because the Dents owned a few dozen slaves, the abolitionist Grants scorned them as lazy and dissolute. Nonetheless, after a prolonged engagement, complicated by the disapproval of Julia's father, the couple married in St. Louis in August 1848. The Grants registered their disapproval by boycotting the wedding altogether.

Long periods of enforced separation marked the courtship and early marriage of Ulysses and Julia Grant, producing an abundant trove of letters from husband to wife. Spelling was a mystery that Grant somehow never mastered and he was no less challenged by grammar, but one can already spy the rudiments of his mature prose style during their four-year courtship, when Grant was stationed in Louisiana and Texas before fighting in Mexico. These early letters have a charming, breathless quality as Grant pines for Julia's presence. In messages heavy with youthful yearning, he tells her "how much anxiety and suspense" he feels as he awaits her letters. The lovelorn soldier assures her that, true to a mutual pledge they made, he thinks of her every day at sunset. "At that time I am most always on parade and no doubt I sometimes appear very absent minded." Grant comes across as a chaste, almost prudish young man, incorrigibly naive, with none of the rough swagger of most soldiers. "No one is so capable of giving good advice as a lady," he informs Julia without apparent irony, "for they always practice just what they would preach."

During their years apart, Grant seemed cruelly suspended in midair, unsure of Julia's intentions. He treasured her letters, hung on her every word, and repeatedly chided her for not writing more often. (We don't know why Julia's letters, fewer in number, have vanished, leaving us with only his side of the correspondence.) Reliant on Julia's love, Grant remained uncertain of its continuance, often lapsing into a sad quandary. "Your letters always afford me a great deal of happiness because they assure me again that you love me still . . . ," he tells her from Texas in a typical passage. He constantly fished for reassurances, alerting Julia on one occasion that he had heard a disturbing rumor that "I have a dangerous rival in Missouri, and that you do not intend to write to me any more."

While in Louisiana and coastal Texas, Grant inhabited a small, circumscribed world and his intensely personal letters were mostly taken up with daydreaming about Julia. Then his regiment penetrated deep into enemy territory, opening his eyes to a larger reality. As his regiment crossed Texas, he had surrendered to the pristine beauty of the countryside, betraying a hitherto unseen sensitivity to nature. "The whole of this country is the most beautiful I ever have seen . . . ," he reported. One senses the wanderlust of a young man who, having grown up in provincial Midwestern towns, now experienced a brand-new universe of sensations in Mexico.

Before he experienced the terror of combat, Grant seemed, in many ways, indistinguishable from other young soldiers aching for home. Then, as the opposing armies clashed, he demonstrates a coolness under fire that foretold his future success in the Civil War. "There is no great sport in having bullets flying about one in evry direction," he informs Julia, "but I find they have less horror when among them than when in anticipation." He explained to her that he had felt no tremor of fear until a cannonball whizzed right past him, knocking off the under-jaw of Captain John Page as he stood nearby. Where others succumbed to terror and confusion, Grant exhibited a preternatural calm and sharp mental focus in battle.

For Grant, the horrors of warfare paled beside the atrocious conduct he witnessed off the battlefield. As he contemplated such action, a fundamental decency surfaced in him. In Matamoros, he bristled at the shameful murder of Mexican civilians by American troops. "Some of the volunteers and about all the Texans seem to think it perfectly right to impose upon the people of a conquered City to any extent, and even to murder them where the act can be covered by the dark. And how much they seem to enjoy acts of violence too!" Where warfare coarsened the sensibility of other soldiers, it brought out in Grant a latent nobility and stubborn sense of fair play. He refused to neglect the human cost of war. After victorious American troops marched into Mexico City, he apprises Julia that "the most astonishing victories have crowned the American arms." Then he rushes to caution her: "But dearly have they paid for it! The loss of officers and men killed and wounded is frightful." During the American occupation of the city, Grant brooded on the blatant inequalities of Mexican society, proving a thoughtful observer with an instinctive sympathy for the underdog. "The rich keep down the poor with a hardness of heart that is incredible."

During the next phase of his life, Grant was again often separated from Julia as he was stranded at a series of frontier outposts. When stationed in Detroit and in Sackets Harbor in upstate New York, he had to endure extended periods alone and his letters to Julia grew plaintive. From Detroit, he assures her, "you know dearest without *you* no place, or home, can be very pleasant to me." And he bitterly missed Fred, their recently born first son. "Does the little dog run about yet?"

he asks Julia before voicing his inmost fear: "I expect he wont know me when he sees me again."

In Detroit and Sackets Harbor, Julia could at least join her husband for extended intervals, mitigating his loneliness. Then he was posted to a pair of bleak garrisons in Oregon Territory and northern California that condemned him to total isolation from his family. His army pay didn't allow him to bring Julia and Fred to the West Coast and he also feared they wouldn't survive the hazardous journey, which required a dangerous passage across the Isthmus of Panama between long ship voyages. On these distant army outposts heavy drinking was the norm and Grant's lonely ordeal drove him to the bottle. "My Dear Wife," he writes from Fort Humboldt in northern California. "You do not know how forsaken I feel here!" He grew his beard several inches long, sat in his room and read during snowbound winter months, and became progressively more miserable. Finally he resigned his commission in April 1854. While Grant maintained that he only wanted to rejoin his family, many in the army believed the story that he had been threatened with a court martial for being drunk while on duty.

From that time until the outbreak of the Civil War, Grant, in St. Louis, failed at one business after another, including farming and real estate, and ended up, in desperation, taking a job as a junior clerk in his father's leather goods store in Galena, Illinois. But at last he was now with his beloved wife and their four children. The flow of letters to Julia dried up during this period altogether only to turn into a torrent when Grant went off to fight the Civil War.

The years of business setbacks didn't diminish Grant's self-confidence, much less destroy it. In wartime, the man abruptly meshed with his historic moment, blowing away the clouds of depression that had trailed him. When the Confederacy fired on Fort Sumter in April 1861, Grant still had the old army lessons from West Point stored in his head, coupled with the broad experience he had gained during the Mexican-American War, when he had not only seen combat but had also served as the regimental quartermaster and commissary. Not long after the fighting started, Grant became a colonel of volunteers and his letters to Julia took on a new, crisply decisive tone. His sterling qualities—modesty, patriotism, integrity, determination, decisiveness, and quiet competence—began to shine through, and he expressed great pride as he whipped his regiment into shape. "I dont believe there is a more orderly set of troops now in the volunteer service," he tells Julia. "I have been very strict with them and the men seem to like it. They appreciate that it is all for their own benefit."

Grant's wartime letters chart his rise in the army and his growing confidence in his capacity for high command. However much he missed Julia, he carried an enormous burden of work and often urged her to stay away. "I am in most excelent health, work all the time scarsely ever geting a half hour to ride out on horseback," he reports from Cairo, Illinois, his early base on the Mississippi River. As a result, Julia was fated to a nomadic life during the war, sometimes joining Grant at his various headquarters, at other times staying with her widowed father in St. Louis or with Grant's parents in Covington, Kentucky. This pattern explains why certain battles, such as Fort Donelson and Shiloh, are well documented in this volume, while others, such as the Confederate surrenders at Vicksburg and Appomattox, are absent.

Even amid the horror and carnage of war, we can see Grant taking pride in his accomplishments. This supremely modest man allowed himself to brag a little. As he wrote to Julia after the fall of Fort Donelson in Tennessee, "This is the largest capture I believe ever made on the continent. . . . This was one of the most desperate affairs fought during this war." Grant had always suffered from his overbearing father and now that he was made a major general, he wryly asks Julia, "Is father afraid yet that I will not be able to sustain myself?"

Grant's wartime letters are concise and economical as befit a busy man with little leisure for rambling commentary. Nevertheless, each letter contains some arresting nugget of information or unexpected glimpse into Grant's thinking. He displays a preference for relentless movement, saying the best way to avoid bloodshed "is to push forward as vigorously as possible." Unlike many of Lincoln's whining, procrastinating generals, Grant comes across as uncomplaining and self-sufficient. "Whatever is ordered I will do independantly and as well as I know how." Amid the constant jockeying for power among Union generals, Grant proves a model of professional restraint. "I am pulling no wires, as political Generals do, to advance myself." There are also plenty of humorous touches here, as when Grant, near Vicksburg, bemoans that his servant has accidentally thrown out his dentures with a basin of water. And no matter how swamped he was with work, Grant never neglected to inquire after his children's health and studies.

As in his letters to Julia during the Mexican-American War, Grant provides carefully edited glimpses of the gruesome fighting, evoking for Julia the "incessent fire of musketry and artillery" at Shiloh. But he also shows a deep humanity, devoting passages to civilian suffering. As his army approaches Corinth in northern Mississippi, he notes the town's desolation, with its broken windows and destroyed furniture. "Soldiers who fight battles do not experience half their horrors," he says to Julia, telling of the many families who have fled. "All the hardships come upon the weak, I cannot say innofensive, women and children."

Letters tend to conceal as much as they disclose and Grant is largely silent about his lifelong struggle with alcohol.

Nonetheless, now and then, the reader discerns how the widespread drinking allegations leveled against Grant preyed on his mind. After Shiloh, he assures Julia, "We are all well and me as sober as a deacon no matter what is said to the contrary." When he is sent a bottle of bourbon as a present, Grant makes a point of reassuring Julia that he transferred it to his friend, General William Tecumseh Sherman. "Myself nor no one connected with the staff ever tasted it."

Another recurrent theme of the letters is Grant's burgeoning awareness of the evils of slavery and his passionate concern for the thousands of fugitive slaves who flocked to his camps. At the start of the war Julia still owned slaves, and in the spring of 1862 Grant urged her to free them, saying that it wasn't "probable we will ever live in a slave state again" and that he didn't care to see the slaves "sold under the hammer."

The bloody horrors of the war only worsened in its later stages, with Grant constantly at the center of events. During the siege of Vicksburg, he described for Julia how he fired shells at the city every few minutes so that its inhabitants "are kept continuously in their caves." He told her of his "desperate effort" to break the siege of Union forces at Chattanooga and open a new supply line for his famished soldiers. After he became general-in-chief in March 1864 and made his headquarters in the field with the Army of the Potomac in Virginia, the war descended to some of its most nightmarish moments. From Spotsylvania he insisted to Julia that "the world has never seen so bloody or so protracted a battle as the one being fought and I hope never will again."

Despite the backdrop of constant bloodshed, perhaps the dominant theme of these wartime letters is Grant's unyielding optimism about the outcome. As he awaited the fall of Petersburg and Richmond in early April 1865, he wrote, "I am feeling very well and full of confidence"—a faith in success that seldom deserted him during the war. But after Lincoln's assassination, instead of being able to relax at last, Grant found himself grappling with a troubled peace. He was still general-in-chief and the postwar problems that pressed in upon him were no less vexing than the wartime ones. "I find my duties, anxieties, and the necessity for having all my wits about me, increasing instead of diminishing," he wrote ruefully to Julia less than two weeks after Appomattox. The pressures on him only intensified during Reconstruction and his two-term presidency as he dealt with the unfinished business of the war.

As a coda to this volume, the editors have added a touching farewell letter that Grant wrote to Julia on June 29, 1885, as he lay dying in a cottage atop Mount McGregor in upstate New York. He said that he would have preferred to be buried at West Point, except that Julia could not lie beside him there for eternity. She chose instead the Upper West Side of Manhattan, where they now occupy twin sarcophagi in Riverside Park. During her widowhood, Julia proposed to Mark Twain that he publish a selection of her husband's letters to her. Twain never followed through, but the editors at Library of America have belatedly proven the wisdom of her inspired idea.

Part I

☆ ☆ ☆

June 4, 1844
to
February 2, 1854

☆ ☆ ☆

Camp Salubrity
Near Nachitoches Louisiana
June 4th 1844

My Dear Julia

I have at length arrived here with the most pleasing recollections of the short leave of absence which prevented my accompanying my Regiment; and as well, with the consequences of the leave. I arrived here on Monday the 3d Ins; I believe just the day that I told you I thought I should arrive. My journey to N. Orleans was a pleasant one, on a pleasant boat, with pleasant passengers and officers, but was marked with no incident worth relating, except that as we approached the South the Musquetoes become troublesome, and by the time I left N. Orleans my hands and face bore the strongest testamony of their numbers and magnitude.—I spent something over a day in N. Orleans, and its being a tolerably large place, and my Bump of Acquisitiveness[1] prompting me on to see as much of the place as possible, the result was that I went over the town just fast enough to see nothing as I went, stoped long enough at a time to find out nothing atall and at the end found myself perfectly tired out. But I saw enough to convince me that a very pleasant season might be passed there; and if I *cant* get back to *Jeff. Bks* again will make no objections to the contemplated change which sends me there. But I am not disposed to give up a known good for an untried one, and as I *know* the climate

[1]A reference to phrenology, in which different "bumps" in the skull are believed to reveal specific character attributes.

&c. (&c. meaning much more than what precedes it) about St. Louis suits me well, I will by no means fail to take up with any offer which will take me back.—My journey up the Red River was not so pleasant as the other. The boat was quite small and considerably crouded with passengers, and they not of the most pleasant sort; a number of them being what are usually called *Black Legs* or Gamblers; and some of them with very cut throat appearances. There was some of them that I should very much dislike to meet unarmed, and in a retired place, their knowing I had a hundred dollars about me. Likely I judge harshly. The monotony of the Journey though was somewhat broken by the great difference in the appearance of the Red River country and anything else I had ever seen. The first hundred miles looks like a little deep and winding canal finding its way through a forest so thickly set, and of such heavy foliage that the eye cannot penetrate. The country is low and flat and overflown to the first limbs of the trees. Aligators and other revolting looking things occupy the swamps in thousands; and no doubt the very few people who live there shake with the ague all Summer. As far up the river as where we are the land is high and healthy, but too poor to bear any thing but one vast pine forest. Since Mr. Hazlitt[2] wrote to you our Encampment has been moved to a much more pleasant and higher situation. We are on the top of a high ridge, with about the best spring of water in Louisiana runing near. There is nothing but pine woods surrounding us and they infested to an inormaus degree with Ticks, Red bugs, and a little creeping thing looking like a Lizard, that I dont know the name of. This last vermin is singularly partial to society, and become so very intimate and sociable on a short acquaintance as to visit our tents, crawl into our beds &c. &c. Tis said they are very innocent but I dont like the looks of

[2]Grant's West Point classmate, Second Lieutenant Robert Hazlitt (c. 1821–1846).

them.—Nearly the first person I met here was Hazlitt, or Sly Bob, with one of those Stage driver's round top wool hats and a round jacket, trying to take the heat as comfortably as possible. He drew me into his tent; which by the way is a little linen affair just like your Fishing tent, with the ground covered with Pine leaves for a floore. It took me one day to answer his questions, and you may rest assured that a number of them were about Ellen[3] and yourself together with the rest of the family. When you write to him tell him how Clarra is comeing on.—Since I first set down to write we have had a hard shower and I can tell you my tent is a poor protection. The rain run through in streams. But I will have a shed built in a few days then I will do better. You have been to Camp Meeting, and know just how the people cook, and sleep, and live there? Our life here is just about the same. Hazlitt probably told you all about how we live here. While I think of it he sends his love to you and Ellen and the rest of the family, and to Wrenshall Dent's[4] family. Mine must go to the same.—

I was detained a day longer in St. Louis than I expected and to make time pleasantly pass away I called on Joe Shurlds[5] and had a long talk of three or four hours, about—about!—let me see: What was the subject? I believe it was the usual topic. Nothing in particular, but matters generally. She pretends to have made a great discovery. Can you concieve what it was?

Julia! I cannot express the regrets that I feel at having to leave Jeff. Bks. at the time that I did. I was just learning how to enjoy the place and the *Society*, at least a part of it. Blank

—— —— —— —— —— —— —— —— —— ——

—— —— —— —— —— —— —— —— —— ——

—— —— —— Read these blank lines just as I intend them and they will express more than words.—You must not forget

[3]Ellen (Nellie) Wrenshall Dent (1828–1904), Julia's younger sister.
[4]George Wrenshall Dent (1819–1899), Julia's older brother.
[5]Josephine Shurlds (1827–1910), George Wrenshall Dent's sister-in-law.

to write soon and what to seal with. Until I hear from you I shall be,—I dont know what I was going to say—but I recon it was your most humble and Obt. Friend.

ULYSSES S GRANT

P.S. Did you get the Magazines I sent you, one from Memphis the other from N. Orleans? usg

Camp Necessity La.
Grand Ecore & Texas Road
Aug. 31st 1844

My Dear Julia

Your two letters of July and August have just been recieved and read you can scarsely immagine with how much pleasure. I have waited so long for an answer to my three letters (I have written you three times Julia one of them you probably had not time to get when you wrote yours) that I began to dispare of ever recieving a line from you; but it come at last and how agreeable the surprise! Take example in punctuality by me Julia, I have rec'd your letters only to day and now I am answering them. But I can forgive you since the tone of your last letter, the one in pencil, is so conclusive of constancy. I am sorry to hear that Mrs. Dent[6] thinks there is nothing serious in our engagement with me nothing is more serious or half as pleasant to think of—Since the arrival of your letters I have read them over and over again and will continue to do so until another comes. I have not been into Camp Salubrity yet to

[6]Ellen Wrenshall Dent (1792–1857), Julia's mother.

deliver to Mr. Hazlitt verbally the messages you sent him, but I wrote him a note this morning containing them. Mr. Hazlitt has been quite unwell for a few days past—You probably have heard from Mr Porters[7] letters that for the last three weeks my company have been road making—The day we came out it rained very hard all day—the men had heavy Knap sacks to carry through the mud and rain for a distance of about five miles and no shelter to go under at the end of their journey—My fare was just the same only I had nothing but myself to carry—The first night we had to lay our wet beds on the still damper ground and make out the best we could—Muskctoes and Wood ticks by the hundreds pestered us—On the whole I spent a few miserable nights and not much better days at the begining of my first experience at campaigning, but now I find it much better—We will probably be through and return to Camp Salubrity in ten days more—I have just rec'd a letter from Fred[8], he is about my most punctual correspondent, he speaks of Louise Stribling. I think she certainly is not married nor wont be unless she gets Fred—Fred is very well but hartily tired of Fort Towson—He proposes that him and me should each get a leave of absence next Spring and go to Missouri I would accept his proposal but I intend going sooner—I shall try very hard to go in the Fall—The happiness of seeing you again can hardly be realized, and then like you I have so much that I would like to say and dont want to write.—Julia do tell me the secrets that Georgia M[9] disclosed to you—I think I can guess them from what follows in your letter—Georgia

[7]Theodoric Henry Porter (1817–1846), a second lieutenant in Grant's regiment, the 4th Infantry.
[8]Frederick T. Dent (1820–1892), Julia's older brother and Grant's West Point classmate.
[9]Georgia Morrison (1829–1884), daughter of Captain Pitcairn Morrison (1795–1887) of the 4th Infantry.

M is a very nice modest and inexperienced girl and can very easily be made to believe anything her oldest sister tells her—I know very well that Fanny[10] has told her that I was in love with her and she foundes her reasons for thinking so upon what took place at you house—You remember the occurrence of the apple seeds? Fany has tried to find out from Mr. Hazlitt which I loved best Georgia or Julia—Mr. Hazlitt would not tell her which he thought because to please her he wou—ld have to tell what he believed to be a story, and to have said you (as he believed though of course he new nothing about certain) he thought would give an unnecessary offense. Hazlitt told me of the conversation he had and it displeased me so much with Miss F. that I said things of her which I would not commit to paper—Believe me my dear Julia what ever Miss Georgia may have told you she no doubt believed herself, but in believing she has allowed herself to be the dupe of one older than she is, but whose experience *in love affairs*, ought to be worth a great deel more than it is.—Tell me what she said in your next letter—Dont let Mrs. Dent see this part of my letter for of all things I dont like to have to speak ill of a third person, and if I do have to speak so I would like as few as possible to know it.—I am very far from having forgotten our promise to think of each other at sun seting—At that time I am most always on parade and no doubt I sometimes appear very absent minded—You say you were at a loss to ascribe a meaning to the blank lines in my first letter! Nothing is easyer, they were only intended to express an attachment which words would fail to express   Julia do not keep anything a secret from me with persons standing in the relation that we do to each other there should be no backwardness about making any request—You commenced to make a request of me and checked yourself—Do not be affraid

[10]Fanny Morrison (1826–1884), Georgia's older sister.

that any thing you may request will not be granted, and just think too the good you might do by giving good advice—No one is so capable of giving good advice as a lady, for they always practice just what they would preach—No doubt you have laid down to Fred. just the course he ought to take, and if he follows the advice he must do well—How fortunate he must feel himself to have a sister to correspond with I know I should have been proud to have had such a one to write to me all the years of my absence. My oldest sister[11] is old enough to write now and I intend to direct all my home letters to her—She loves you and Ellen already without ever having seen you just from what she has heard me say—You say Julia that you often dream of me! do tell me some of your good ones; dont tell me any more of the bad ones; but it is an old saying that dreams go by contraries so I shall hope you will never find me in the condition you drempt I was in—And to think too that while I am writing this the ring I used to wear is on your hand—Parting with that ring Julia was the strongest evidence I could have given you (that is—in the way of a present) of the depth and sincerity of my love for you—Write to me soon, much than the last time and if Mrs. Porter[12] is not there, or not writing at the time take a little ride and put your letter in the Post Office—On the road think of some of the conversations we used to have when we rode out together

Most Truly and Devotedly Your Lover
ULYSSES

P S I think in the course of a few days Julia I will write to Col. Dent[13] to obtain his consent to our correspondence; I will ask

[11]Clara Rachel Grant (1828–1865).
[12]Elizabeth Lloyd Beall Porter (1827–1850), the wife of Theodoric Henry Porter.
[13]Frederick F. Dent (1787–1873), Julia's father. The military title was honorific.

nothing more at present but when I get back to St. Louis I will lay the whole subject before him Julia do not let any disclosed secrets such as Miss Georgia told you, make you doubt for a moment the sincerity depth & constancy of my feeling, for you and you alone out of the whole acquaintance. Find some name beginning with "S" for me Julia You know I have an S in my name and dont know what it stand for.

U.S.G.

P.P.S. Tell Ellen that I have not been into Camp yet to see the playthings she sent Mr. Hazlitt but I will go tomorrow morning if I have to walk. I think there is no danger of us quarreling since we have agreed so long together; but if we do get into a scrape I will let her know it. Remember me to Miss Ellen, Mrs. Porter Mrs. Mary Dent[14] and your Fathers family all.

USG

Camp Salubrity La
Near Nachitoches
Sept. 7th 1844

My Dear Julia

I have just written the letter you desired I should, and which I have long thought it a duty to write. You can scarsely concieve the embarrassment I felt in writing such a letter, even in commencing the first line. You must not laugh at it Julia for you have the chance I send it unsealed that you may read it before

[14]Mary Isabella Shurlds Dent (1824–1909), the wife of George Wrenshall Dent.

delivering it. I wrote it at our little camp in the woods on the road to Texas while alone by my self, at night. I immagined all the time that I saw your Pa & Ma. reading it and when they were done, raising all kinds of objections. Youth and length of acquaintance I feared might be brought against us but assure them my dear Julia that the longest acquaintance, or a few years more experience in the world could not create a feeling deeper or more durable. While I have been writing this there has been three or four officers in the tent bothering and talking to me all the time but they have just gone out thank fortune. They do not suspect that I am writing to you. It has only been a few days since I received your letters. I answered them immediately, wont you be as punctual in answering mine in the future? You dont know Julia with how much anxiety and suspense I await there arrival. But here I am asking you to write soon and in the same letter asking permission to have you write, and without knowing that the favor will be granted. If the proper consent is obtained I know you will follow the example of punctuality I have set.

I wrote to Fred a day or two ago: I told him I would accept his invitation to go to Mo. next Spring if I did not go sooner, but at present the prospect is so fair for the 4th Regiment going to Jefferson Barracks to spend next winter that I am in hopes that shorter leaves will be long enough for me to visit Gravois.[15] You dont know how much I want to get back there once more. Another of our little walks up or down the creek would be so pleasant, and then too you could tell me what you say you want to tell and cant write. In your next wont you tell me all about the secrets Miss Georgia made known to you. I do assure you Julia that you need not let anything she can tell you, about me, give the least trouble.

[15]White Haven, the Dent plantation, was located on Gravois Creek.

Mrs. Capt. Page and Mrs. Alden have each written to their husbands that they saw General Scott[16] lately and he says that he intends sending our Regiment up the Mississippi as soon as possible; and if he does we will get to Jeff. Bks. about November where we will have to stay until the river breaks up above which will be about next May. It is now about Eleven o'clock P. M. and Mr. Porter and me are each sitting writing letters to go to Gravois. All the time I am writing mine I am thinking that probably Julia has on, the ring that I left her, and who knows but just at this time she may be dreaming of me! How much I flatter myself dont I? to think that your thoughts might be upon me during your sleep.

Mr. Porter is through writing his letter and waiting to get this to seal them up. You know he is Post Master? He says that when you write to me again you must put a little cross on the outside that he may know the letter is for me. The last one he opened before he found it out—Mr. Hazlitt I believe I told you has been sick. His health is improving gradually, but he is very tired of this country. He says he does not consider it living atall; but merely spining out an existance. He desires to be remembered to you and Ellen and the rest of the family. He has never seen any of the play things yet that Ellen sent him. Possibly they will be here to-morrow for I understand that Mr. Wallen's[17] baggage is just arriving. Mr. Hazlitt says he wishes you would write him just one letter—Remember me to all the people at Gravois little Davy[18] and all.

ULYSSES

[16]Major General Winfield Scott (1786–1866), general-in-chief of the U.S. Army, 1841–61.

[17]Second Lieutenant Henry D. Wallen (1819–1886) of the 4th Infantry.

[18]David O. Porter, the infant son of Theodoric Henry Porter.

P. S. Julia dont let any one but your Pa. & Ma read the letter I have directed to them will you?

U

Camp Salubrity
Near Nachitoches La.
January 12th 1845

My Dear Julia

It has now been nearly two months since I heard from you and about four since I wrote the letter to your parents to which I hoped so speedy an answer. Of course I cannot argue any thing very strong in favor of my request being granted from their not answering it, but at the same time they do not say that I shall not write to you, at least as a friend, and therfore I write you this Julia, and direct it to Sappington P. O. expecting your Pa & Ma to know that you get it. The fact is I thought I must hear from you again—The more than ordinary attachment that I formed for *yourself* and family during my stay at Jeff. Bks. cannot be changed to forgetfulness by a few months absence. But why should I use to you here the language of flattery Julia, when we have spoken so much more plainly of our feeling for each other? Indeed I have not changed since and shall hope that you have not, nor will not, at least untill I have seen all of you once more. I intend to apply for a leave in the spring again and will go to St. Louis. For three months now I have been the only officer with my company and of course cannot leave even for one week. Julia can we hope that you pa will be induced to change his opinion of an army life? I think he is mistaken about the army life being such an unpleasant one. It is true the movements of the troops from Jeff. Bks. so suddenly and to so outlandish a place would rather create that opinion, but then such a thing hardly occurs once a lifetime.

Mr. Hazlitt returned about one month ago looking as lazy and healthy as ever. I was away from camp when he returned and did not get home until about midnight. I woke him up and him and me had a long talk from that until morning. He told me all about what a pleasant visit he had at Jeff. Bks. or rather on the Gravois. Was he plagued much about Miss Clara while there? You dont know how much I wished to be along with him! He regrets very much that he didnot return by St Louis.—I must tell you something about Mr. Hazlitt since he returned. He has got him a little pony about the size of the one I had at Jeff. Bks. it is a little "Jim a long Josy"[19] of a thing and if you were to see it you would think it was going to drawl out "*y-e-s im* hisn" just as you know Mr. Hazlitt does himself; he rode his pony to a Ball four or five mile from camp a few days ago and as he was joging along the road, neither pony nor man thinking of anything I suppose, the little thing stumbled and away went Hazlitt over its head rolling in the dust and dirt. When he got up he found the pony laying with its head in the other direction so it must have turned a complete summer-set. I was not at the Ball myself, and therefore didnot see Hazlitts exhibition and it was several days before he told me of it. He could'nt keep it a secret. You ought to be here a short time to see how we all live in our winter houses. They are built by puting posts in the ground as if for a fence and nailing up the outside with shingles. I have plank for my house but there is but one or two other officers that have. The chimneys are of mud and sticks and generally are completed by puting a barrel

[19]The title of a minstrel song (1840) by Edward Harper.

or two on top to make them high enough. Mr. Porter, Wallen, & Ridgley have built themselves fine houses expecting their families here. Mr. Porter went three or four weeks ago to visit his wife [ ][20] the mouth of Red river. If they were here they might live very pleasantly for the weather is so warm that we need but little or no fires. Mr. Hazlitt and me keep bachilors hall on a small scale and get along very pleasantly. We have an old woman about fifty years old to cook for us and a boy to take care of our horses so that we live as well as though we were out of the woods—Mr. Hazlitt wishes to be remembered to all of you. He says that you must write to him right off.—I hear from Fred. very often. He was well the last time he wrote. Julia you must answer this quick wont you? I know you can. Give my love to all the family

Fare well
ULYSSES

Camp Salubrity
Near Nachitoches La.
Tuesday, May 6th 1845

My Dear Julia

I have just arrived at Camp Salubrity after a tolerably pleasant trip of only one week from St. Louis, with one days detention at the mouth of Red River. I am here just in time; one day later I would have probably an excuse to write. Whilst at the mouth of Red river I met with Lt. Baker who is strait from Fort Towson. He left there only about one week ago. Fred. is very well, and would have been in Missouri with me

[20]A bracketed space [ ] is used in this book to indicate where words are missing or illegible as a result of damage to the manuscript of a letter.

but his commanding officer refused him a leave. It was right mean in him was'nt it?—Evry thing at Camp Salubrity Looks as usual only much greener from the contrast between the advancement of the season here and in the North. Though we are so far South and vegetation so far advanced a fire this evening is very comfortable. The officers are all collected in little parties discussing affairs of the nation. Annexation of Texas, war with Mexico, occupation of Orregon and difficulties with England[21] are the general topics. Some of them expect and seem to contemplate with a great deal of pleasure some difficulty where they may be able to gain laurels and *advance a little in rank*. Any moove would be pleasant to me since I am so near promotion that a change of post would not affect me long. I have advanced three in rank very lately, leaving only five between me and promotion.—Mr. Hazlitt has gone to Fort Jesup and wont be back for a week; he left this morning before I got here.—It seems very strange for me to be siting here at Camp Salubrity writing to you when only a little more than one short week ago I was spending my time so pleasantly on the Gravois.—Mrs. Porter started a few days ago for Washita and of course took little Dave. along so that I could not give him the kiss you sent him. Mr. Porter was very particular in his enquiries about all of you, and if he knew that I was writing would send his love. When I got to Nachitoches I found Mr. Higgins[22] and Beaman there just ready to start on a leave of absence. I am sorry that Miss Fanny dont know that he is on the way. I wanted him to tell me if he intended to bring her to Salubrity with him but he would not say yes nor no. Tell me what the probabilities are.—Have you heard yet from Col.

[21]Congress voted to annex Texas on March 1, 1845. The Anglo-American dispute over the northwestern border was resolved by a treaty signed on June 18, 1846.

[22]Second Lieutenant Thaddeus Higgins (1817–1845) of the 4th Infantry.

Dent?[23] I supose Brand must have written you a very amusing account of his adventures in the East.—I supose Capt. Cotton has taken Lizzy to Green Bay before this. Does John pretend to be as much as ever in love?—The first thing I did after geting here was to get my letters from the Post Office. I found one from Miss J. B. D. that afforded me a great deel of pleasure, and one from home that had come by the way of St. Louis.—Is Miss Jemima Sappington married yet?—Tell John not to take it so hard as he appeared inclined to when he first heard of it.—I wrote to Fred. on my way down the Mississippi and told him of the pleasant visit I had, and how disappointed you all were that he was not along. I shall always look back to my short visit to Mo. as the most pleasant part of my life. In fact it seems more like a pleasant dream than reality. I can scarsely convince myself of the fact that I was there so short a time ago. My mind must be on this subject something like what Hercules Hardy's was whilst he was a prisoner among the Piannakataws in Guiana. I send you the story[24] that you may read it.—Remember me very kindly to Mrs. Dent and Ellen and Emmy and your brothers and to your Aunt Fielding[25] and your Cousins. Dont neglect to write as soon as you get this.

I am most devotedly your
ULYSSES S. GRANT

P. S. I promised to write to Lewis Dent[26] as soon as I got here but I am so busily engaged building myself a new house that I

[23]John Cromwell Dent (1816–1889), Julia's older brother.
[24]*The Adventures of Hercules Hardy, or: Guiana in 1772* (translated 1844) by French novelist Eugène Sue (1804–1875).
[25]Emily (Emmy) Marbury Dent (1836–1920), Julia's youngest sister; Sarah Wrenshall Fielding (1800–1855), Julia's aunt.
[26]Lewis Dent (1823–1874), Julia's older brother.

will not have much time for a while. Mrs. Wallen[27] is here safe and looks very delicate.—I am going to follow your advice Julia and have me a good and comfortable house.

U.

The letter you wrote me before I went to Mo. was very different from what I expected to find it. It was not near so cold and formal as you led me to believe. I should not have written this last Post script should I?

u

N. Orleans Barracks La.
July 11th 1845

My Dear Julia

I wrote you a letter a few days ago in which I promised to write again by Mrs. Wallen. It was my intention then to write you a very long one but she starts much sooner than I expected so that I will only trouble you with a short note, and it too will probably reach you before the letter sent by Mail. There is now no doubt Julia but we will all be in Texas in a very short time. The 3d Infantry have arrived on their way and in a week or so we will all be afloat on the Gulf of Mexico. When I get so far away you will still think of and write to me I know and for my part I will avail my self of evry opportunity to send you

[27] Laura Louisa DeCamp Wallen (1827–1915), the wife of Henry D. Wallen.

a letter. It cannot well be many months that I will be detained in that country unless I be promoted to one of the Regiments stationed there and the chances are much against that. I have never mentioned any thing about *love* in any of the letters I have ever written you Julia, and indeed it is not necessary that I should, for you know as well as I can tell you that you alone have a place in my *my*—What an out I make at expressing any thing like love or sentiment: You know what I mean at all events, and you know too how acquerdly I made known to you for the first time my love. It is a scene that I often think of, and with how much pleasure did I hear that my offer was not entirely unacceptable? In going away now I feel as if I had some one els than myself to live and strive to do well for. You can have but little idea of the influance you have over me Julia, even while so far away. If I feel tempted to do any thing that I think is not right I am shure to think, "Well now if Julia saw me would I do so" and thus it is absent or present I am more or less governed by what I think is your will.

Julia you know I have never written anything like this befor and wont you keep any one from seeing it. It may not be exactly right to keep it from your parents, but then you will get a letter from me by Mail about the same time which they will probably see. Am I giving you bad advice? if you think so act just as you think you ought.—Mrs. Wallen will give you all the news afloat here. Dont forget to ask her how she intends to direct her letters to Mr. Wallen and send mine to the same address, and now I must close with sending the most devotional love of

U S G

N. Orleans Barracks La.

My Dear Julia

I wrote to you several days ago expecting that Mrs. Wallen would start the next day for St. Louis and would be the bearer of my letter, but at the time that she expected to get off she was taken sick and has not been able to start until now, so my Dear Julia I write you a second sheet hoping that any addition to one of my letters will be as agreeable to you as a Post Script to one of your letters is to me. Since I wrote you the first sheet several things of importance, or at least new, have taken place. One company of Artillery is now between this and the mouth of the Mississippi river to join us for Texian service. Mr. and Mrs. Higgins[28] have arrived and appear to be as happy as you please. Mrs. Higgins for some time persisted in accompanying her husband into the field but she has at length given it up.— Something melancholy has taken place too. On the evening of the 15th Inst. Col Vose,[29] for the first time since I have been in the Army, undertook to drill his Regiment. He was probably some what embarrassed and gave his commands in a loud tone of voise; before the drill was over I discovered that he put his hand to his breast when ever he commenced to give any command, and before he was through with the parade he was compelled to leave the field and start for his qarters, which were hardly fifty paces off, and just upon arriving there he fell dead upon the poarch. He was buried to-day (July the 15th)[30] with millitary honors.

That evening late I was sent to town to have the Obituary notice published; the next evening I was sent again to have

[28]Fanny Morrison Higgins.

[29]Josiah H. Vose (1784–1845), commander of the 4th Infantry since 1842.

[30]Vose died on July 15, 1842, and was buried on July 17.

the order and time of the funeral put in the papers and was returning between 1 and 2 o'clock at night when I discovered a man and woman that I thought I knew, footing it to the city carrying a large bundle of clothes. I galloped down to the Barracks to ascertain if the persons that I suspected were absent or not and found that they were. I was ordered immediately back to apprehend them, which by the assistance of some of the City Watchmen I was able to do. I had the man put in the watch house and brought the *lady* back behind me on my horse to her husband, who she had left asleep and ignorent of her absence. Quite an adventury was'nt it?

Mrs. Higgins and husband have arrived just in time to find us *en route* for Texas. I believe she will return to Jeff. Bks. in a day or two. She brings news Julia which if I did not believe she was mistaken in would give me some trouble of thoughts. She says that I have a dangerous rival in Missouri, and that you do not intend to write to me any more &c. &c. Of course Julia I did not believe this, yet the fact of any one saying it was so gave me some uneasiness. I knew, or at least thought I knew, that even if any thing of the kind was so that you would let me know it and not tell it to a disinterested person. I am right in this am I not? You must not think Julia that I have been questioning and pumping to get the above information; it was voluntarily given and not to me but to another who come and told me. You will write to me soon wont you and contridict the above statement. Mrs. Higgins told me to-day that she would carry any letters or packages that I might have to send you. I will send these by Mrs. Wallen and when the other asks me for my letters I will tell her that I understand that you do not intend writing to me any more and of course cant expect me to be writing to you. If you direct your letters to me at N. Orleans La. or Corpus Christi Texas they will be forwarded to where I am. This makes five letters I have written you since I was in

Mo. wont you in turn write me one immediately and another in two or three weeks after? Give my love to all your fathers and your Aunt Fieldings families.

Yours affectionately
U S GRANT

P. S. We will start for Texas in the course of three or four days. While you are reading this I will be thinking of you at Corpus Christi, that is if so fortunate as to get there safely. In a few months I shall hope to be back promoted. I now have but three now between me and promotion; a few months ago I had nine or ten, dream of me Julia and rest assured that what I have heard has not weight enough to chang my love for you in the slightest.

U S G to Julia
July 17, 1845

☆ ☆ ☆

Corpus Christi Texas
Sept. 14th 1845

My Dear Julia

I have just recieved your letter of the 21st ultimo in which you reproach me so heavily for not writing to you oftener. You know my Dear Julia that I never let two days pass over after recieving a letter from you without answering it; But we are so far separated now that we should not be contented with writing a letter and waiting an answer before we write again. Hereafter I will write evry two or three weeks at farthest, and wont you do the same Julia? I recieved your letter before the last only about three weeks ago and answered it immediately. Your letters always afford me a greatdeal of happiness because they assure me again that you love me still; I never doubted your love Julia for one instant but it is so pleasant to hear it repeated, for my own part I would sacrifice evrything Earthly to make my Dear Julia my own forever. All that I would ask would be that my Regiment should be at a healthy post and you be with me, then I would be content though I might be out of the world. There are two things that you are mistaken in Julia, you say you know that I am in an unhealthy climate and in hourly expectation of War: The climate is delightful and very healthy, as much so as any climate in the world and as for war we dont believe a word of it. We are so numerous here now that we are in no fear of an attack upon our present ground. There are some such heavy storms here on the coast the later part of Sept. and October however that we will probably be moved up the Nuices river to San Patricio, an old deserted town, that the Indians have compelled the inhabitants to leave.—Since the troops have been at Corpus Christi there has not been a single death from sickness, but there has been two or three terrible visitations of providence. There has been one man drownd in the breakers; a few weeks ago a storm passed over camp and a flash of lightning struck a tent occupied by two black boys killing one and stuning the other, and day before yesterday the most terrible accidents of all occured. For the last few weeks there has been an old worn out Steam Boat, chartered by government, runing across the bay here, and day before yesterday there happened to be several officers and a number of soldiers aboard crossing the bay; the boat had scarsely got out of sight when the boilers bursted tearing the boat into atoms and througing almost evry one aboard from twenty to fifty yards from the wreck into the Briny Deep. Some were struck with iron bars and splinters and killed immediately others swam and got hold of pieces of the wreck and were saved. Among the killed was Lt. Higgins and Lt. Berry both of the 4th Infantry. It will drive Fanny almost mad I fear. Capt. Morrison takes Mr. Higgins' death very hard. When he was killed he was standing talking with several officers; the others were uninjured. The number killed and wounded I have not heard accurately stated, but I believe there was 9 killed and about 17 wounded one or two probably mortally.

Do you hear much about War with Mexico? From the accounts we get here one would supposed that you all thought the Mexicans were devouring us. The vacancies that have lately occured brings me about first for promotion and if by chance I should go back to the States I may have the pleasure of seeing my Dear Julia again before the end of the year; what happiness it would be to see you again so soon! I feel as though my good fortune would take me back. If I should be promoted to a Regt. in Texas I will have to remain untill na[ ] affairs look a little more settled and we become permanent in this country, which is a delightful one so far as climate and soil is concerned, but where no one lives scarsely except the troops, and then I will go back and either remain there, or—May I flatter myself that one who I love so much would return with me to this country, when all the families that are now absent join there husbands?—If so Julia you know what I would say.

The mail is just going to close so I must stop writing. I intended to have written another sheet but I will have to put off my long letter until next time. Give my very best love to all your family and also Mrs. Fieldings. Dont neglect writing to me very soon Julia for you dont know anxious I always am to get a letter from my *Dear Dear* Julia and how disappointed I always feel when I am a long time without one from her. I very often look at the name in the ring I wear and think how much

I would like to see again the one who gave it to me. I must close, so good by my Dear Julia

U S GRANT

Corpus Christi Texas

My Dear Julia

In my last letter I promised to write to you evry two or three weeks and it is now about that time since I wrote and you see how punctual I am. I fear Julia that there was a long time between the receipt of my letters from N. Orleans and my first from Texas but you must reflect that I had writen you three without having recieved an answer and before writing again I wanted to hear from my *Dear Dear* Julia. I always do and always will answer your letters immediately and if you knew how delighted I always am to hear from yourself you would write often too.

The late casualty in the 4th Infantry promotes me so that I am now permanently at home in this Regiment. I should have prefered being promoted to a Regiment that is now in the States, because then I would get to see again, *soon*, one who is much dearer to me than my commission, and because too, there is hardly a probability of active service in this remote quarter of our country, and there is nothing els, excepting a fine climate and soil, to make one wish to stay here.—There is now over half of the Army of the U. States at Corpus Christi, and there must of course be a breaking up and scatterment of this large force as soon as it is found that their services will not be required in this part of the country. It is the general opinion that on account of the length of time the 4th has already been encamped, here and at Camp Salubrity, and the general unsettled position that it has been in since the begining of the Florida war,[31] that we will be the first out of Texas. Once in quarters again no doubt we will remain for a good long time.

The most of the talk of war now comes from the papers of the old portion of the U. States. There are constantly bands of Mexican Smugglers coming to this place to trade, and they seem to feel themselvs as secure from harm here as though they were citizens of Texas, and we on the other hand, although we are occupying disputed Territory, even acknowedging our right to Texas, feel as secure from attack as you do off in Missouri. There was a time since we have been here when we were in about half expectation of a fight and with a fare prospect of being whipped too; that was when there was but few of us here and we learned that General Arista[32] and other officers of rank were on the Rio Grande ready to march down upon us. We began to make preparations to make as stout a defence as possible. Evry working man was turned out and an intrenchment began and continued for about a week and then abandoned.

Now my Dear Julia that a prospect is ahead for some perminancy in my situation dont you think it time for us to begin to settle upon some plan for consumating what we believe is for our mutual happiness? After an engagement of sixteen or seventeen months ought we not to think of bringing that engagement to an end, in the way that all true and constant lovers should? I have always expressed myself willing you know my Dear Julia to resign my appointment in the army for the sake of overcomeing the objections of your parents, and I would

[31]The Second Seminole War, 1835–42.

[32]Mariano Arista (1802–1855), commander of the Mexican Army of the North.

still do so; at the same time I think they mistake an army life very much. No set of ladies that I ever saw are better contented or more unwilling to change their condition than those of the Army; and you Julia would be contented knowing how much and how dearly devoted I am to you—I cannot help writing thus affectionately since you told me that no one but yourself reads my letters.

Your Pa asks what I could do out of the Army? I can tell you: I have at this time the offer of a professorship of mathematics in a tolerably well endowed College in Hillsboro, Ohio, a large and flourishing town, where my salery would probably equal or exceed my present pay. The Principle of the Institution got my father to write to me on the subject; he says I can have until next spring to think of this matter. The last letter I wrote was to make all the enquiries I could about the situation and if the answer proves favorable I shall give this matter serious concideration.

I am now reading the Wandering Jew,[33] the copy that belonged to Mr. Higgins and the very same numbers read by yourself. How often I think of you whilst reading it. I think well Julia has read the very same words that I am now reading and not long before me. Yesterday in reading the 9th No I saw a sentence marked around with a pencil and the word *good* written after it. I thought it had been marked by you and before I knew it I had read it over three or four times. The sentence was a sentiment expressed by the Indian Prince Djalmo on the subject of the marriage of two loving hearts, making a compareison you may recollect.[34] Was it you that marked the place.

[33] *The Wandering Jew* (1844–45) by Eugène Sue.

[34] "Yes, your talk afflicts me, slave—for two drops of dew blending in the cup of a flower are as hearts that mingle in a pure and virgin love; and two rays of light united in one inextinguishable flame, are as burning and eternal joys of lovers joined in wedlock."

I have written so long a letter that I must close. Remember me to evry body on the Gravois. Mr. Hazlitt also wishes to be remembered.

Give my love to Ellen. How is Ellen's soft eyed lover comeing on that she wanted me to quiz somebody down here about? She did not say so but I know she wanted some of her friends here to hear of him just to see how jealous she could make them.

Good bye my Dear Julia and dont forget to write soon.

Yours most affectionately
ULYSSES
October 1845

Corpus Christi Texas
Jan. 2d 1846

My Dear Julia

I have just returned from a tour of one month through Texas, and on my return I find but one single letter from my Dear Julia and that one but a few lines in length. You dont know how disappointed I felt, for in my two or three last letters, which remain unanswered yet, I said something that I was somewhat impatient to recieve an answer too.

On the 2d of Dec. myself and some fifteen other officers started for San Antonio which is about one hundred and fifty miles from here and laying beyond a district of country which heretofore has been rendered uninhabitable by some bands of Indians—The Comanches and others—who have always been the enemies of the white man. Of course we had to camp out during the journey and we had very disagreeable weather to do it in too. Some of the old Texans say they have scarsely ever seen as disagreeable a winter as this one has been. From San Antonio I went across to Austin, the seat of Government. The whole of the country is the most beautiful that I ever have seen, and no doubt will be filled up very rapidly now that the people feel a confidance in being protected. San Antonio has the appearance of being a very old town. The houses are all built of stone and are begining to crumble. The whole place has been built for defence, which by the way was a wise precaution, for untill within three or four years it has been the scene of more blood shed than almost any place of as little importance in the world. The town is compact, the houses all one story high only, the walls very thick, the roofs flat and covered with dirt to the depth of two or more feet they have but few doors and windows and them very small so the town cant be burned down, and a few persons in side of a house can resist quite a number. Austin in importance or at least in appearance is about equal to Carondolett. The inhabitants of San Antonio are mostly Mexicans. They seem to have no occupation whatever.

I have but little doubt Julia but that my Regt. the 4th Inf.y (I was promoted to the 7th but I have transfered to the 4th) will go up the Miss. river in the course of a few months now, but so far as I am concerned myself I dont know but I would prefer remaining in Texas. On you account Julia I would prefer going back but even here I think you would be contented.

Here it is now 1846 Julia, nearly two years since we were first engaged and still a time when or about when our marriage is to be consumated has never been talked of. Dont you think it is now time we should press your father further for his concent? If you would speak to him on the subject I think he would give his concent; you know he told me that you never spoke to him of our engagement and infact would hardly give him a chance to speak to you of it. If you think it best I will write again to him.

You know Julia what I think we would be justifiable in doing if his concent is still witheld and I hope you think nearly with me. Wont you give the matter a serious concideration and tell me soon, very soon if we agree. You alone Julia have it in your power to decide whether in spite of evrything we carry our engagement into effect. You have only to decide for me to act. If you will set a time when I must be in Missouri I will be there no matter if my Reg.t is still in Texas. The matter is one of importance enough to procure a leave of absence, and besides for the love I bear my dear Julia I would not value my commission to highly to resign it. I ought not to commit this to paper where there is danger that it may be seen before you get it, but I cannot help it, it is what I feel and have expressed before. My happiness would be complete if a return mail should bring me a letter seting the time—not far distant—when I might "clasp that little hand and call it mine."

Your Devoted Lover
ULYSSES

Corpus Christi Texas
Feb. 7th 1846

Dearest Julia

I have just been delighted by a long and interesting letter from my Dear Julia and although I wrote to you but two or three days ago I answer this with my usual punctuality. You say you write me letter for letter well I am satisfied that my love is returned and you know how anxious one is to hear often from the one they love and it may appear to me that you do not write as often as you really do. Your letter was one of the sweetest you have ever written me and your answer to the question I have so often asked was so much like yourself, it was just what I wanted to hear you say; boldness indeed: no my Dear Julia that is a charge that can never be laid to you.—There is a part of your letter that is entirely incomprehensible to me. I dont know whether you are jesting or if you are serious. * * *[35] I first loved Julia I have loved no one els.—The chance of any of the troops geting out of Texas this spring is worse than ever, before long we will be on our way farther West but no doubt it will be but a few months until the boundary question will be settled and then we may look for a general dispersion of troops and I for one at least will see Missouri again.—Does your pa ever speak of me or of our engagement? I am so glad to hear you say that you think his consent will be given when asked for. I shall never let an oportuntiy to do so pass.—As to resigning it would not be right in the present state of affairs and I shall not think of it again for the present.—So John is again a Bachilor without a string to his bow. no doubt he will remain single all his life The extract from some newspaper you send me is a gross exageration of the morals and health of Corpus Christi. I do not believe that there is a more healthy spot in the world. So much exposure in the winter season is of course attended with a goodeal of sickness but not of a serious nature. The letter was written I believe by a soldier of the 3d Inf.y. As to the poisning and robberies I believe they are entirely false.

[35]In this book, three asterisks indicate places where Julia Dent Grant later crossed out words or passages in the letters.

There has been several soldiers murdered since we have been here, but two of the number were shot by soldiers and there is no knowing that the others were not. Soldiers are a class of people who will drink and gamble let them be where they may, and they can always find houses to visit for these purposes. Upon the whole Corpus Christi is just the same as any other plase would be where there were so many troops. I think the man who wrote the letter you have been reading deservs to be put in the Guard house and kept there until we leave the country. There he would not see so much to write about.—Do you get the paper I send you evry week?—I know Julia if you could see me now you would not know me, I have allowed my beard to grow two or three inches long. Ellen would not have to be told now that I am trying to raise whiskers. Give my love to all at White Haven.

Your Devoted lover
ULYSSES

Camp Near Matamoras
March 29th 1846

My Dear Julia

A long and laborious march, and one that was threatened with opposition from the enemy too, has just been completed, and the Army now in this country are laying in camp just opposite to the town of Matamoras. The city from this side of the river bears a very imposing appearance and no doubt contains from four to five thousand inhabitants. Apparently there are a large force of Mexican troops preparing to attack us. Last night during the night they threw up a small Breast work of Sand Bags and this morning they have a piece of Artillery mounted on it and directed toward our camp. Whether they really intend anything or not is doubtful. Already they have boasted and threatened so much and executed so little that it is generally believed that all they are doing is mere bombast and show, intended to intimidate our troops. When our troops arrived at the Little Colorado,[36] (a river of about 100 yards in width and near five feet deep where we forded it) they were met by a Mexican force, which was represented by there commander to be large and ready for an attack. A parly took place between Gen. Taylor and their commanding officer, whose name I have forgotten, the result of which was, that if we attempted to cross they would fire upon us. The Mexican officer said that however much he might be prepossessed in our favor himself he would have to obey the orders of his own Government, which were peremptory and left him but one course, and that was to defend the Colorado against our passing, and he pledged his honor that the moment we put foot into the water to cross he would fire upon us and war would commence. Gen. Taylor replied that he was going over and that he would allow them fifteen minuets to withdraw their troop and if one of them should show his head after he had started over, that he would fire upon them; whereupon they left and were seen no more until we were safely landed on this side. I think after making such threats and speaking so positivly of what they would do and then let so fine an opportunity to

[36]A river in the Rio Grande delta that flows into Laguna Madre opposite South Padre Island, Texas.

execute what they had threatened pass unimproved, shows anything but a decided disposition to drive us from the soil. When the troops were in the water up to their necks a small force on shore might have given them a greatdeel of trouble.—During our whole march we have been favored with fine weather, and alltogether the march has been a pleasant one. There are about forty miles between the Nuices and the Colorado rivers that is one continuous sandy desert waste, almost without wood, or water with the exception of Salt Lakes. Passing this the troops of course suffered considerably.—Here the soil is rich and the country beautiful for cultivation. When peace is established the most pleasant Military posts in our country I believe will be on the Banks of the Rio Grande. No doubt you suppose the Rio Grande, from its name and appearance on the map to be a large and magnificent stream, but instead of that it is a small muddy stream of probably from 150 to 200 yards in width and navigable for only small sized steamers. I forgot to mention that we recieved before we arrived here, the proclamation of Col. Majia the Commander-in-Chief I believe, of the Mexican forces. It was a long wordy and threatning document. He said that the citizens of Mexico were ready to expose their bare breasts to the Rifles of the Hunters of the Mississippi, that the Invaders of the North would have to reap their Laurels at the points of their sharpened swords; if we continued our march the deep waters of the Rio Grande would be our Sepulcher the people of our Government should be driven East of the Sabine and Texas re-conquered &c. &c. all of which is thought to mean but very little.

The most beligerent move that has taken place yet occured yesterday. When we had arrived near this place a party of Mexican soldiers siezed upon two of our Dragoons and the horse of a Bugler boy who had been sent in advance to keep an eye in the direction of the enemy and to communicate if they saw any movement towards our column. The prisoners are now confined in the city. It is quite possible that Gen. Taylor will demand the prisoners and if they are not given up march over and take the city or attempt it.

I am still in hopes notwithstand all warlike appearances that in a few months all difficulties will be settled and I will be permitted to see again My Dear Dear Julia. The time will appear long to me until this event but hope that has so long borne me out, the hope that one day we will meet to part no more for so long a time, will sustain me again. Give my love to all at White Haven and be sure to write soon and often. I have not heard from Fred. very lately. Vacancies have occured here which make him I think 2d from promotion and another will probably take place soon in the case of an officer who is to be tried for being drunk on duty.—I will write again in a few days, but dont put of answering this until you get my next.

ULYSSES

Point Isabel Texas
May 3d 1846

My Dear Julia

I wrote you a long letter in answer to your last sweet letter a few days ago and intended to bring it with me to this place but when we started I left in such a hurry that I forgot it. I gave you a long account of our difficulties in it and as I now have but a few minuets to write I will send you the other letter as soon as I get back. At present I can only give you what has happened without any of the circumstances. Col. Cross[37] has been killed by the Mexicans. Capt Thornton with three other officers and about fifty Dragoons fell in with a camp of some two thousand Mexicans and of course were taken. One officer and six or seven men were killed and four wounded all the others were taken prisoners. Lt. Porter with twelve men were attacked by a large number of Mexicans and Mr. Porter[38] and one man was killed the rest escaped.—Gen. Taylor left Matamoras with about two thousand troops for this place on the 1st of May intending to give the Mexicans a fight if we fall in with them. We marched nearly all night the first night and you may depend My Dear Julia that we were all very much fatigued. We start again at 1 o'clock to-day and will probably have an engagement. We understand that there is several thousand encamped not far from this place. There was about six hundred troops left in our Fort opposite Matamoras and the presumption is they have been attacked, for we have heard the sound of Artillery from that direction ever since day light this morning. As soon as this is over I will write to you again, that is if I am one of the fortunate individuals who escape. Dont fear for me My Dear Julia for this is only the active part of our business. It is just what we come here for and the sooner it begins the sooner it will end and probably be the means of my seeing my dear Dear Julia soon. You dont know how anxious I am to see you again Julia. Another year certainly cannot roll round before that happy event. I must now bring my letter to a close. I wish

[37]Colonel Trueman Cross (1796–1846), quartermaster of the Army of Observation commanded by General Zachary Taylor, disappeared while out riding on April 10. His body was found eleven days later.
[38]Theodoric Henry Porter.

I had time to write a much longer one. Give my love to all at White Haven. Write to me soon Julia.

Your Most devoted
U. S. GRANT
4th Inf.y

☆ ☆ ☆

Head Quarters Mexican Army
May 11th 1846

My Dear Julia

After two hard fought battles[39] against a force far superior to our own in numbers, Gen. Taylor has got possesion of the Enemy's camp and now I am writing on the head of one of the captured drums. I wrote to you from Point Isabel and told you of the march we had and of the suspected attack upon the little force left near Matamoras. About two days after I wrote we left Point Isabel with about 300 waggons loaded with Army supplies. For the first 18 miles our course was uninterupted but at the end of that distance we found the Mexican Army, under the command of General Arista drawn up in line of battle waiting our approach. Our waggons were immediately parked and Gen. Taylor marched us up towards them. When we got in range of their Artillery they let us have it right and left. They had I believe 12 pieces. Our guns were then rounded at them and so the battle commenced. Our Artillery amounted to 8 guns of six pound calibre and 2 Eighteen pounders. Evry

[39]The battles of Palo Alto, May 8, and Resaca de la Palma, May 9, 1846.

moment we could see the charges from our pieces cut a way through their ranks making a perfect road, but they would close up the interval without showing signs of retreat. Their officers made an attempt to charge upon us but the havoc had been so great that their soldiers could not be made to advance. Some of the prisoners that we have taken say that their officers cut and slashed among them with their Sabres at a dreadful rate to make them advance but it was no use, they would not come. This firing commenced at ½ past 2 o'clock and was nearly constant from that until Sun down.

Although the balls were whizing thick and fast about me I did not feel a sensation of fear until nearly the close of the firing a ball struck close by me killing one man instantly, it nocked Capt. Page's under Jaw entirely off and broke in the roof of his mouth, and nocked Lt. Wallen and one Sergeant down besides, but they were not much hurt. Capt. Page is still alive.[40] When it become to dark to see the enemy we encamped upon the field of battle and expected to conclude the fight the next morning. Morning come and we found that the enemy had retreated under cover of the night. So ended the battle of the 8th of May. The enemy numbered three to our one besides we had a large waggon train to guard. It was a terrible sight to go over the ground the next day and see the amont of life that had been destroyed. The ground was litterally strewed with the bodies of dead men and horses. The loss of the enemy is variously estimated from about 300 to 500. Our loss was comparitively small. But two officers were badly wounded, two or three slightly. About 12 or 15 of our men were killed and probably 50 wounded. When I can learn the exact amount

[40]Captain John Page (1795–1846) of the 4th Infantry died from his wounds on July 12.

of loss I will write and correct the statements I have made if they are not right. On the 9th of May about noon we left the field of battle and started on our way to Matamoras. When we advanced about six miles we found that the enemy had taken up a new position in the midst of a dense wood, and as we have since learned they had recieved a reinforcement equal to our whole numbers. Grape shot and musket balls were let fly from both sides making dreadful havoc. Our men continued to advance and did advance in spite of their shots, to the very mouths of the cannon and killed and took prisoner the Mexicans with them, and drove off with their own teams, taking cannon ammunition and all, to our side. In this way nine of their big guns were taken and their own ammunition turned against them. The Mexicans fought very hard for an hour and a half but seeing their means of war fall from their hands in spite of all their efforts they finally commenced to retreat helter skelter. A great many retreated to the banks of the Rio Grande and without looking for means of crossing plunged into this water and no doubt many of them were dround. Among the prisoners we have taken there are 14 officers and I have no idea how many privates. I understand that General Lavega, who is a prisoner in our camp has said that he has fought against several different nations but ours are the first that he ever saw who would charge up to the very mouths of cannon.

In this last affray we had we had three officers killed and some 8 or ten wounded. how many of our men suffered has not yet been learned. The Mexicans were so certain of sucsess that when we took their camp we found thir dinners on the fire cooking. After the battle the woods was strued with the dead. Waggons have been engaged drawing the bodies to bury. How many waggon loads have already come in and how many are still left would be hard to guess. I saw 3 large waggon loads at one time myself. We captured, besides the prisoners, 9 cannon, with a small amount of ammunition for them, probably 1000 or 1500 stand of fire arms sabres swords &c. Two hundred and fifty thousand rounds of ammunition for them over four hundred mules and pack saddles or harness. Drums, musical instruments camp equipage &c, &c. innumerable. The victory for us has been a very great one. No doubt you will see accounts enough of it in the papers. There is no great sport in having bullets flying about one in evry direction but I find they have less horror when among them than when in anticipation. Now that the war has commenced with such vengence I am in hopes my Dear Julia that we will soon be able to end it. In the thickest of it I thought of Julia. How much I should love to see you now to tell you all that happened. Mr. Hazlitt come out alive and whole. When we have another engagement, if we do have another atall, I will write again; that is if I am not one of the victims. Give my love to all at White Haven and do write soon my Dear Julia. I think you will find that history will count the victory just achieved one of the greatest on record. But I do not want to say to much about it until I see the accounts given by others. Dont forget to write soon to your most Devoted

ULYSSES

P. S. I forgot to tell you that the Fortifications left in charge of Maj. Brown in command of the 7th Inf.y was attacked while we were at Point Isabel and for five days the Mexicans continued to throw in shells. There was but 2 killed, Maj. Brown & one soldier, and 2 wounded.

Matamoras Mexico
July 2d 1846

My Dear Julia

I recieved last evening your letter of the 10th of June, in which you speak of this Earthly paradise. If it is a Paradise where it rains about four hours each day why then Matamoras is the place. I have no doubt though I should like the place very much if it was only the home of My Dearest Julia, but I know that I shall never be contented until I am with her once more. I am afraid Julia that Matamoras will be very sickly this Summer. The whole of this country is low and flat and for the last six weeks it has rained almost incessantly so that now the whole country is under water. Our tents are so bad that evry time it rains we get a complete shower-bath. I dont believe that we will leave here for two or three months and then we will either have some hard fighting or bring our difficulties in this quarter to a speedy close. Now that the Oregon boundary is no longer in dispute I think we will soon quiet Mexico and then dearest Julia, if I am not one of the unfortunate who fall, nothing will keep me from seeing you again. I really am very much in hopes that an other Spring will not roll around before I will be able to call Julia my own dear, (shall I say wife,) Just think it is now going on three years since we were first engaged! You never will tell me Julia if you think your Pa & Ma will say no. I dont think they can but I would like to hear you say that they will not.—I did not let the flowers in your last letter blow away. When I opened the letter and saw the rose leaves I just thought that only two short weeks ago Julia had them in her own hands and here I am and have not seen her fore more than a year. If I was in Mo. and you were here I know what I would do very soon; I would volunteer to come to Mexico as a private if I could come no other way. But I recollect you did volunteer some time ago, or what showed your willingness to do so, you said that you wished we had been united when I was last in Mo. and how willing you would be to share even a tent with me. Indeed Julia that letter made me feel very happy. How much I ought to love you when you express a willingness to sacrifice so much just for me.—I believe you have burned some of my letters for you say you only have twenty five of them and it seems to me I have written a great many more; at all events I will write more in the future and you must write often too wont you Julia? So you have read that rediculous falsehood about the cause of Lt. Deas[41] crossing the river. There was not a word of truth in the whole statement except that he swam the river. It was a strange fancy that struck him at a time when he was not duly himself. Fred. has not got here yet. I wonder what can keep him? I shall pick a quarrel with him as soon as he gets here for not writing to me. He is a great deal worse than you are about writing; but I ought not to say a word about your writing now for you are so much more punctual than you used to be. I will write to you again in a few days but you must not wait to get another letter before you answer this. I would like to make a bargain for each of us to write, say, evry Sunday [ ] then just think I would hear from my Dear love fifty two times in a year. Remember me to all at White Haven.

Your Devoted
ULYSSES

[41]First Lieutenant Edward Deas (c. 1822–1849) swam across the Rio Grande on April 13 and was captured. Some newspapers reported that he was searching for Colonel Cross, while others claimed that he was smitten with a Mexican woman. Deas was freed in a prisoner exchange on May 11, 1846.

P. S. You say that I must not let Fred. read your letters. I know now how to get you to write often. Evry time that two weeks elapse without geting a letter from my Dearest Julia I will just take out one of the old ones and give it to Fred. to read. You had better look out and write often if you dont want him to read them.

U S GRANT

P. P. S. Since writing the above I have heard that Fred is in N. Orleans on his way here. I suppose he will be here in two or three days. I'll make him write to you as soon as he comes.

Matamoras Mexico
July 25th 1846

My Dearest Julia

It must be about two weeks since I have written to you, and as I am determined that a longer time shall never pass with my Dearest hearing from me, whilst I am in an enemie's country, I write to you again, notwithstanding I have not heard from you for some time. Do not understand me though to cast any censure upon you, for you may have written me a dozen letters and me not recieved one of them yet, for I believe it is about two weeks since we have had a Mail, and there is no telling when we will have another. You must not neglect to write often Dearest so that whenever a mail does reach this far-out-of-the-way country I can hear from the one single person who of all others occupies my thoughts. This is my last letter from Matamoras Julia. Already the most of the troops have left for Camargo and a very few days more will see the remainder of us off. Whether we will have much more fighting is a matter of much speculation. At present we are bound for Camargo and from thence to Monteray, where it is reported that there is several thousand Mexican troops engaged in throwing up Fortifications, and there is no doubt either but that Parades[42] has left Mexico at the head of nine thousand more to reinforce them, but the latest news says that he has been obliged to return to the City of Mexico on account of some rupture there. But a few months more will determine what we have to do, and I will be careful to keep my Dear Julia advised of what the army in this quarter is about. Fred. has not arrived here yet but I am looking for him daily. His commission arrived some time ago, and also a letter from St. Louis for him. I have them both in my possession, and wrote to him to hasten on. His Reg.t. (the 5th Infantry) is already in Camargo. A few months more of fatigue and privation, I am much in hopes, will bring our difficulties to such a crisis that I will be able to see you again Julia, and then if my wishes prevailed, we would never part again as merely engaged, but as,—you know what I would say.—No doubt a hard march awaits us between Camargo and Monteray. The distance is over two hundred miles, and as I have understood, a great part of it without water. But a person cannot expect to make a Campaign without meeting with some privations.

Fred. and me will probably be near each other during the time and between us I am in hopes that I will hear from my Dear Julia evry week, but write oftener to me than to Fred.—Since we have been in Matamoras a great many murders have been committed, and what is strange there seemes to be but very week means made use of to prevent frequent repetitions.

[42]General Mariano Paredes y Arrillaga (1797–1849) became interim president of Mexico on January 4, 1846. Paredes was overthrown by an insurrection in Mexico City on August 4.

Some of the volunteers and about all the Texans seem to think it perfectly right to impose upon the people of a conquered City to any extent, and even to murder them where the act can be covered by the dark. And how much they seem to enjoy acts of violence too! I would not pretend to guess the number of murders that have been committed upon the persons of poor Mexicans and our soldiers, since we have been here, but the number would startle you.—Is Ellen married yet? I never hear you mention her name any more. John I suppose is on his way for the seat of war by this time.[43] If we have to fight we may all meet next winter in the City of Mexico.

There is no telling whether it will be as prisoners of war or as a conquering force. From my experience I judge the latter much the most probable.—How pleasant it would be now for me to spend a day with you at White Haven. I envy you all very much, but still hope on that better times are coming. Remember me to all at White Haven and write very soon and very often to

ULYSSES

Camp Near Monteray Mex.
Sept. 23d 1846

My Dear Julia

It is now after night and an opportunity occurs of sending a letter tomorrow to where it can be mailed, and you know my Dear Julia I told you I would not let a single chance escape of

[43]Julia's brother John Cromwell Dent was an officer in the 2nd Missouri Mounted Volunteers and served in New Mexico.

writing to you. If I could but see you I could tell you a volume on the subject of our last three days engagement, but as I write this I am laying on the ground with my paper laying along side in a very uneasy position for any one to give a detailed account of battles so you must be satisfied with a simple statement of facts, and the assurance that in the midst of grape and musket shots, my Dearest Julia, and my love for her, are ever in my mind. We have indeed suffered greatly but sucsess seems now certain. Our force is but six thousand that of the enemy is probably much greater, but is not known. The siege of Monteray was commenced on the 20th Ins. but we did not fire our first gun until the morning of the 21st. Monteray is a city of from six to ten thousand inhabitants. The houses are all low and built of stone. In the town and on all the commanding points the Mexicans have erected fortifications and seem determined to fight until the last one is taken by shere force. Already all those on the high points of ground have been taken and many Mexican lives with them. We are now playing upon them with pieces of Artillery and ammunition that we have captured but they still hold their citadel and Artillery enough to man it. Our loss has been very great, particularly in the 3d & 4th Inf.y. The killed and wounded officers runs as follows (leaving out a number of Volunteers who I do not know the names of.)

1st Inf.y Capt. Lamotte an arm off, Lt. Terrett badly wounded and in the hands of the Mexicans, Lt. Dillworth lost a leg. 3d Inf.y Capt. Morris, Capt. Field Maj. Barbour, Lt. Irwin & Lt. Hazlitt killed Maj. Lier severely wounded, the ball passing in at the nose and out at the ear. His recovery doubtful. 4th Inf.y Lt. Hoskins & Lt. Woods killed and Lt. Graham severely wounded. In the other Regt. there was more or less killed or wounded but the loss not so severe. I passed through some severe fireing but as yet have escaped unhurt

Of course My Dear Julia if I get through (and I think the severest part is now over) I will not let an opportunity of writing to you escape me. I have not had a letter from you since we left Matamoras which was on the 5th of August but I know there must be one or two on the way some place I am geting very tired of this war, and particularly impatient of being separated from one I love so much, but I think before I see another birth day I shall see Julia, and if she says so, be able to call her my own [ ] Dear for ever. It is about time for me to close writing until Monteray is entirely ours, so give my love to all at White Haven and write very soon to

ULYSSES

Camp Near Monteray Mex.
Oct. 3d 1846

My Dearest Julia

I wrote to you while we were still storming the city of Monteray and told you then that the town was not yet taken but that I thought the worst part was then over. I was right for the next day the Mexicans capitulated and we have been ever since the uninterupted holders of the beautiful city of Monteray. Monteray is a beautiful city enclosed on three sides by the mountains with a pass through them to the right and to the left. There are points around the city which command it and these the Mexicans fortified and armed. The city is built almost entirely of stone and with very thick walls. We found all their streets baricaded and the whole place well defended with artillery, and taking together the strength of the place and the means the Mexicans had of defending it it is almost incredible that the American army now are in possession here. But our victory was not gained without loss. 500, or near abouts, brave officers and men fell in the attack. Many of them were only wounded and will recover, but many is the leg or arm that will be buryed in this country while the owners will live to relate over and over again the scenes they witnessed during the siege of Monteray. I told you in my last letter the officers that you were acquainted with that suffered, but for fear the letter may not reach you I will inumerate them again. Capt. Morris of the 3d Inf.y Maj. Barbour Capt. Field Lt. Irwin Lt. Hazlitt Lt. Hoskins and Lt. Terrett & Dilworth since dead. Lt. Graham & Maj. Lier dangerously wounded. It is to be hoped that we are done fighting with Mexico for we have shown them now that we can whip them under evry disadvantage. I dont believe that we will ever advance beyond this place, for it is generally believed that Mexico has rec'd our Minister and a few months more will restore us to amity. I hope it may be so for fighting is no longer a pleasure. Fred. has not joined us yet and I think it a great pity too, for his Regiment was engaged at a point where they done the enemy as much harm probably as any other Reg.t but lost but very few men and no officer. Monteray is so full of Orange Lime and Pomgranite trees that the houses can scarsly be seen until you get into the town. If it was an American city I have no doubt it would be concidered the handsomest one in the Union. The climate is excellent and evry thing might be produced that any one could want * * * I have written two pages and have not told you that I got a letter a few days ago from my Dear Dear Julia. It has been a long long time since I got one before but I do not say that you have not written often for I can very well conceive of letters loosing their way following us up. What made you ask me the question Dearest Julia "if I thought absence could conquer love"? You ought to be just as good a judge as me! I can only answer for myself alone, that Julia is as *dear* to me to-day as she was the day we visited St. Louis together, more than two years ago, when I first told her of my love. From that day to this I have loved you constantly and the same and with the hope too that long before this time I would have been able to call you *Wife*. Dearest Julia if you have been just as constant in your love it *shall not* [   ] long until I will be entitled to call you by the [   ] affectionate title. You have not told me for a long time Julia that you still loved me, but I never thought to doubt it. Write soon to me and continue to write often. Now that we are going to stay here some time I am in hopes that I will get a number of letters from you. I forgot to tell you that by the terms of the capitulation the Mexicans were to retire beyond Linariz within seven days and were not to fight again for eight weeks and we were not to advance for the same time. Fred. certainly will join soon and then I will make him write often. Give my love to all at White Haven

ULYSSES

P. S. I am going to write to you evry two weeks if I have an opportunity to write so you may know if you dont get letters that often that some of them are lost

U.

Camp Near Monteray Mex.
Oct. 20th 1846

My Dear Julia

How very very lonesome it is here with us now. I have just been walking through camp and how many faces that were dear to the most of us are missing now. Just one month ago this night the 4th Inf.y left this camp not to return again until it had lost three of its finest officers. (Lt. Graham has since died) I came back to my tent and to drive away, what you call the Blues, I took up some of your old letters, written a year or so ago and looked them over, I next took up a Journal[44] that I kept whilst at Jefferson Barrack and read as far as to where I had mentioned "that of late I could read but very little for I was so busy riding about and occationally visiting my friends in the country—who by the way are becoming very interesting." That part Julia must have been written about the time I first found that I loved you so much. It brought the whole matter to mind and made me think how pleasantly my time passed then. It seems very hard that I should not be able now to spend a few days in the year as I did then evry week. How long this state of things is to continue is yet a problem but it is to be hoped not long. When you walk down the branch to Aunt Fieldings do you ever think of our walks on that road? How very often they come to my mind. This is my third letter since the battles to you Julia so that if you dont hear from me often it is not my fault.— * * *

We occationally get reports here that negociations are going or that proposals of the kind have been made by this Government. I hope sincerely that such is the case for I am very

[44]The journal is not known to have survived.

anxious to get out of the country. This is the most beautiful spot that it has been my fortune to see in this world, but without you *dearest* a Paradice would become lonesom.—Fred. is not with us yet and I am now giving up the hope of seeing him here. I have had his commission for a long time and the other day I concluded to send it to him. One or two of the Mails comeing this way from Camargo have been robed lately and the letters sent to Gen. Ampudia and by him to Gen. Santa Ana. Ampudia was polite enough to inform Gen. Taylor of the fact.—Before you get this no doubt there will be great excitement in the states in concequence of the battle of Monteray, and no doubt you will hear many exaggerated accounts of the valorous deeds performed by individuals. I begin to see that luck is a fortune. It is but necessary to get a start in the papers and there will soon be deeds enough of ones performances related. Look at the case of Capt. Walker![45] The papers have made him a hero of a thousand battles.—Give my love to all at White Haven and write to me very soon. I would like to know Julia if your Father ever says or hints a word on the subject of our engagement?

Farewell my Dearest until my next letter which will be in a week or two

Your Devoted
ULYSSES

P. S. The Mail has not left here since writing the above. All are well except many slight cases of Fever & Ague. Capt. Ridgely of the Artillery, whose name no doubt you have often seen in print, met with a severe accident yesterday, the 26th He

[45]Samuel Hamilton Walker (1817–1847) of the Texas Rangers.

was riding through Monteray and his horse fell with him and fractured his scull. His life is dispaired of.

U

Castle of Perote Mexico
April 24th 1847

My Dear Julia

You see from the above that the great and long talked of Castle of Perote is at last in the hands of the Americans. On the 13th of this month the rear Division of Gen. Scott's army left Vera Cruz to drive Santa Anna and his army from the strong mountain passes which they had fortified, with the determination of driving back the Barbarians of the North, at all hazards. On the morning of the 17th our army met them at a pass called Cierra Gorda a mountain pass which to look at one would suppose impregnable. The road passes between mountains of rock the tops of which were all fortified and well armed with artillery. The road was Barricaded by a strong work with five pieces of artillery. Behind this was a peak of the mountains much higher than all the others and commanded them so that the Enemy calculated that even if the Americans should succeed in taking all the other hights, from this one they could fire upon us and be out of reach themselvs. But they were disappointed. Gen. Twiggs' Division worked its way around with a great deel of laibor and made the attack in the rear. With some loss on our side and great loss on the part of the Enemy this highest point was taken and soon the White flag of the enemy was seen to float. Of Generals and other officers and soldiers some

Six thousand surrendered as prisoners of war Their Artillery ammunition supplies and most of their small arms were captured. As soon as Santa Anna saw that the day was lost he made his escape with a portion of his army but he was pursued so closely that his carriage, a splendid affair, was taken and in it was his cork leg and some Thirty thousand dollars in gold. The pursuit was so close that the Mexicans could not establish themselvs in another strong pass which they had already fortified, and when they got to the strong Castle of Perote they passed on leaving it too with all of its artillery to fall into our hands. After so many victories on our part and so much defeat on the part of the Mexicans they certainly will agree to treat. For my part I do not believe there will be another fight unless we should pursue with a very small force.—From Vera Cruz to this place it is an almost constant rize Perote being about Eight thousand feet above the ocean. Around us are mountains covered with eternal snow and greatly the influance is felt too. Although we are in the Torrid zone it is never so warm as to be uncomfortable nor so cold as to make a fire necessary. From Vera Cruz to this place the road is one of the best and one that cost more laibor probably than any other in the world. It was made a great many years ago when Mexico was a province of Spain. On the road there a great many specimens of beautiful table land and a decided improvement in the appearance of the people and the stile of building over any thing I had seen before in Mexico. Jalapa is decidedly the most beautiful place I ever saw in my life. From its low Latitude and great elevation it is never hot nor never cold. The climate is said to be the best in the world and from what I saw I would be willing to make Jalapa my home for life with only one condition and that would be that I should be permitted to go and bring my Dearest Julia.—The 5th Inf.y, Fred's Reg.t was was not present at the fight of Cierra Gorda. A few days before we left Vera

Cruz the 5th Inf.y was ordered down the coast to Alvarado to procure horses and mules for the use of the army, and when we left they had not returned. My Dearest Julia how very long it seems since we were together and still our march is onward. In a few days no doubt we will start for Puebla and then we will be within from Eighty to a Hundred miles of the City of Mexico; there the march must end. Three years now the 4th Inf.y has been on the tented field and I think it is high time that I should have a leave of absence. Just think Julia it is now three long years that we have been engaged. Do you think I could endure another years separation loving you as I do now and believing my love returned? At least commission and all will go in less time or I will be permitted to see the one I have loved so much for three long years. My Dearest dont you think a soldiers life a hard one! But after a storm there must be a calm. This war must end some time and the army scattered to occupy different places and I will be satisfied with any place wher I can have you with me. Would you be willing to go with me to some out-of-the-way post Dearest? But I know you would for you have said so so often.—Your next letter will probably reach me in Puebla the 3d city in size in the Republic of Mexico. Write to me often Julia I always get your letters. I will write again as soon as the army makes another halt Has your pa ever said anything more about our engagement? You know in one of your sweet letters you told me something he had said which argued that his consent would be given. Remember me affectionately to you father and mother Miss Ellen & Emmy.

ULYSSES

P. S. Among the wounded on our side was Lt. Dana very dangerously. In the Rifle Reg.t one officer, Lt. Ewell, was killed Mr. Maury lost his hand Mason and Davis a leg each. A great many Volunteer officers were killed and wounded. I have not had a letter from you since the one I answered from Vera Cruz but there have been but few mails arrived since. I hope to get one soon.

U

City of Mexico
September 1847

My Dearest Julia

Because you have not heard from me for so long a time you must not think that I have neglected to write or in the least forgotten one who is so ever dear to me. For several months no mail has gone to Vera Cruz except such as Editors of papers send by some Mexican they hire and these generally fall into the hands of the enemy who infest the whole line from here to the sea coast. Since my last letter to you four of the hardest fougt battles[46] that the world ever witnessed have taken place, and the most astonishing victories have crowned the American arms. But dearly have they paid for it! The loss of officers and men killed and wounded is frightful. Among the wounded you will find Fred's name but he is now walking about and in the course of two weeks more will be entirely well.[47] I saw Fred. a moment after he received his wound but escaped myself untouched. It is to be hoped that such fights it will not be our

[46]The battles of Contreras, August 19–20, 1847; Churubusco, August 20; Molino del Rey, September 8; and Chapultepec, September 13.
[47]Frederick T. Dent was wounded in the leg at Molino del Rey.

misfortune to witness again during the war, and how can be? The whole Mexican army is destroyed or disbursed, they have lost nearly all their artillery and other munitions of war; we are occupying the rich and populace valley from which the great part of their revenues are collected and all their sea ports are cut off from them. Evry thing looks as if peace should be established soon; but perhaps my anxiety to get back to see again my Dearest Julia makes me argue thus. The idea of staying longer in this country is to me insupportable. Just think of the three long years that have passed since we met. My health has always been good, but exposure to weather and a Tropicle Sun had added ten years to my apparent age. At this rate I will soon be old.—Out of all the officers that left Jefferson Barracks with the 4th Infantry but three besides myself now remains with us, besides this four or five who joined since, are gone. Poor Sidney Smith was the last one killed. He was shot from one of the houses after we entered the city.

Mexico is one of the most beautiful cities in the world and being the capital no wonder that the Mexicans should have fought desperately to save it. But they deserve no credit. They fought us with evry advantage on their side. They doubled us in numbers, doubled us and more in artillery, they behind strong Breast-works had evry advantage and then they were fighting for their homes. * * * It * * * truly a great country. No country was ever so blessed by nature. There is no fruit nor no grain that cant be raised here nor no temperature that cant be found at any season. You have only to choose the degree of elevation to find perpetual snow or the hotest summer. But with all these advantages how anxious I am to get out of Mexico. You can redily solve the problem of my discontent Julia. If you were but here and me in the United States my anxiety would be just as great to come to Mexico as it now is to get out.

Oct. 25th At last a mail is to leave here for the U States I am glad at finally having an opportunity of leting you hear from me. A train is going to Vera Cruz and with it many of the wounded officers and men. Fred. is geting too well to be one of them. I am almost sorry that I was not one of the unfortunates so that now I could be going back. It is to be hoped that in future mails will be much more frequent though in fact it is generally believed that as soon as congress meets the whole army will be ordered from this valey of Mexico. There is no use of my teling you any more that I will take the first opportunity of geting back to Mo. for I have told you that so often, and yet no chance has occured. At present Gen. Scott will let no officer leave who is able for duty not even if he tenders his resignation. So you see it is not so easy to get out of the wars as it is to get into them.—Write to me often dearest Julia so if I cant have the pleasure of sending letters often to you let me at least enjoy the receipt of one from you by evry Mail coming this way.—No doubt before this the papers are teaming with accounts of the different battles and the courage and science shown by individuals. Even here one hears of individual exploits (which were never performed) sufficient to account for the taking of Mexico throwing out about four fifths of the army to do nothing. One bit of credit need not be given to accounts that are given except those taken from the reports of the different commanders.

Remember me my Dearest Julia to you father & mother and the rest of the family and pray that the time may not be far distant when we may take our walks again up and down the banks of the Gravois. Truly it will be a happy time for me when I see that stram again.

Farewell My Dearest Julia
U S GRANT

☆ ☆ ☆

Tacabaya Mexico
January 9th 1848

My Dear Julia

Since I wrote to you last one Brigade has moved to this place which is about four miles from the City of Mexico and from being so much higher than the City is much more healthy. One Brigade has gone to Toluca and it is rumored that before a great while we will move to some distant part, either Queretero, Zacetecus, San Louis Potosi or Guernivaca unless there is a strong probability of peace. It is now however strongly believed that peace will be established before many months. I hope it may be so for it is scarsely suportible for me to be separated from you so long my dearest Julia. A few weeks ago I went to the commanding officer of my Regiment and represented to him that when the 4th Inf.y left Jefferson Barracks, three years ago last May, I was engaged, and that I thought it high time that I should have a leave of absence to go back. He told me that he would approve it but I found that it would be impossible to get the Comd.g Gen. to give the leave so I never made the application. I have strong hopes though of going back in a few months. If peace is not made it is at all events about my turn to go on recruiting service. As to geting a sick leave that is out of the question for I am never sick a day. Mexico is a very pleasant place to live because it is never hot nor never cold, but I believe evry one is hartily tired of the war. There is no amusements except the Theatre and as the actors & actresses are Spanish but few of the officers can understand them. The better class of Mexicans dare not visit the Theatre or associate with the Americans lest they should be assassinated by their own people or banished by their Government as soon as we leave. A few weeks ago a Benefit was given to a favorite actress and the Govorner of Queretero hearing of it sent secret spies to take the names of such Mexicans as might be caught in indulging in amusements with the Americans for the purpose of banishing them as soon as the *Magnanimous Mexican Republic* should drive away the Barbarians of the North. I pity poor Mexico. With a soil and climate scarsely equaled in the world she has more poor and starving subjects who are willing and able to work than any country in the world. The rich keep down the poor with a hardness of heart that is incredible. Walk through the streets of Mexico for one day and you will see hundreds of begars, but you never see them ask alms of their own people, it is always of the Americans that they expect to recieve. I wish you could be here for one short day then I should be doubly gratified. Gratified at seeing you my dearest Julia, and gratified that you might see too the manners and customs of these people. You would see what you never dreamed of nor can you form a correct idea from reading. * * * All gamble Priests & civilians, male & female and particularly so on Sundays.—But I will tell you all that I know about Mexico and the Mexicans when I see you which I do hope will not be a great while now. Fred. is in the same Brigade with me. I see him evry day. He like myself is in excellent health and has no prospect of geting out of the country on the plea of sickness.—I have one chance of geting out of Mexico soon besides going on recruiting service. Gen. Scott will grant leaves of absence to officers where there is over two to a Company. In my Reg.t there are three or four vacancies which will be filled soon [ ] and will give an oportunity for one or two now here to go out. Give my love to all at White Haven and do not fail to write often dearest Julia. I write but seldom myself but it is because a mail but seldom goes from here to the sea coast. Coming this way it is different for the Volunteers are constantly arriving.

When you write next tell me if Mrs. Porter and Mrs. Higgins are married or likely to be.

Adieu My Dearest Julia
ULYSSES

Tacubaya Mexico
May 7th 1848

Dearest Julia

I have not recieved a letter from you for two months or more until two days ago, but when one did come it was most welcom. It has been a good while since I wrote to you but I can easily explain the reason. On the 3d of April I started with a party to go to the top of Popocatapetl the highest mountain in North America. From the mountain a portion of us went across into the Valley of Cuernavaca to visit the great mammoth cave of Mexico. On this trip I was absent from Mexico sixteen days and in the mean time a mail went off. The day after my return another mail started but I did not hear of it until I saw it leaving, so you see my dearest Julia you cannot attach any criminality to my apparent neglect. What must I think of you. just think two long months without hearing from one that I love so much. * * * Well I do not blame you * * * so long as you dont forget me and love me as you say you do.

There is a great deal of talk of peace here now. The knowing ones say that the Mexican Congress will ratify the terms proposed and that the advance of the American Army will be on its way for Vera Cruz in three weeks. I atleast hope dear

Julia that it will not be long before I can see you again. It is too bad aint it? just think we have been engaged almost four years and have met but once in that time, that was three years ago.

I see Fred almost evry day. I told him what you desired me to. Fred read me a little of Miss Ellen's letter * * *

The trip to the snow mountain and to the cave was very pleasant and would have been more so had we succeeded in geting to the top, but the weather was so unfavorable that all failed. The day that we arrived at the foot of the mountain we ascended about one half of the way to the top and there encamped for the night. We had been there but a short time when it began to blow rain, hale & snow most terrificaly and of course we were in bad plight next morning for ascending a mountain which is difficult at best Next morning however we started through a snow storm which had continued from the night before and the wind blowing hard enough almost to carry a person away. The snow on the mountain drifted so rapidly that it was impossible to see over thirty or forty yards in any direction so we lost the view that we would have had of the surrounding valleys. We ploded on for several hours through all these difficulties when all found that it was perfect madness to attempt to go farther, so we turned back when about 1000 feet below the Crater. That night about the time we were going to lay down, first one person would complain of his eyes hurting him then another and by 9 o'clock evry one was suffering the most excrusiating pain in the eyes. There was but little sleeping done by the party that night. Next morning nine of the officers were blind so that they were obliged to have their horses led One day however restored evry one so far that it was determined not to give up the expedition We then divided, a portion waiting for a favorable day succeeded in reaching the top of the Mountain, the rest of us passing over a low ridge commenced descending and after twenty miles of gradual descent arrive in tierra Calliente, or hot county, Here much to our surprise on approaching quite a large town we were halted by some Mexican officers who forbid our entring the place. The commander said that the place was occupied by Mexican troops and by the terms of the Armistice we were obliged to content our selvs out side of town that night. We met troops at three other places before we reached the cave. They showed no hostile feeling but were very punctillious in their observance of the armistice. The fact is they wanted to annoy us by making us go around without seeing their towns. Traveling through tierra Calliente is a beautiful and strange sight to a Northerner. All seasons of the year you will find vegetation in full bloom. We passed some of the most beautiful sugar Plantations in the world and finest buildings in the world. They beat any in Louisiana. Evry one has on it fine coffe fields and orchards of Tropical fruits such as oranges Bananas and twenty kinds of fruit that I never heard of until I came to Mexico. I have written so long that I must close with telling you that after six days travel from the snow Mountain through this beautiful valley we arrive at the great cave of Mexico and explored it to a considerable distance. The cave is exceedingly large and like the Mammoth cave of Kentucky its extent has never been found out. Some of the formations are very singular. One would think that they were works of art. We had with us torches and rocketts and the effect of them in that place of total darkness was beautiful.

Give my love to all at home. Dont forget to write often. Two months is too long to wait for a letter from one that I love so much.

Adieu My Dear Dear Julia
ULYSSES

P. S. I would take another sheet and give you a more minute discription of my trip but there is an officer waiting, very impatiently for me to get through and go to town where I am obliged to. Dont neglect to write very soon and very often Dearest Julia

Tacubaya Mexico
June 4th 1848

My Dearest Julia

I wrote you a letter about two weeks ago saying that I should not probably ever write to you again from this part of Mexico. But as there is a Mail going in a few days, and it will probably go faster than the troops will march, I will write to you again and for the last time, from here. Peace is at last concluded and the most of the troops are on their way to Vera Cruz. On Thursday next the last of the troops in the Valley of Mexico will leave and I think by the 25th or 30th of July I may count on being in St. Louis. The thought of seeing you so soon is a happy one dearest Julia but I am so impatient that I have the *Blues* all the time. A great many of the business people, in fact nearly all of them, want to see us remain in the country. Already a revolution is looked for as soon as our backs are turned. People who have associated with the Americans are threatened with having their ears & noses cut off as soon as their protectors leave. Gen. Terrace of the Mexican army lives here in Tacubaya with his family. He has five daughters young ladies who are very sociable with officers of the U. S. Army. A few weeks ago an Aid-de-Camp of Gen. Velasco threatened to mark their faces as soon as we left. The threat reached the ears of one of the officers who was in the habit of visiting the young ladies and he gave the valient A. D. C. who was going to make war against innocent females, a good thrashing in a public place, and much to the amusement of the by-standers. Already some barbarities have been committed such as shaving the heads of females, and I believe in one or two cases they cut their ears off. * * * Yesterday an officer had his horse saddle and bridle stolen in broad day light and from the very dencest part of the city. Such thefts are very common. I most hartily rejoice at the prospect of geting out of Mexico though I prefer the country and climate to any I have ever yet seen.

I am going to write you but a short letter dearest Julia because I expect to start at the same time this does. Our march to Vera Cruz I fear will be attended with much fatigue and sickness. Already the rainy season is begining to set in and at Vera Cruz there has been several cases of Yellow fever. Evry precaution will be taken to keep the troops from geting sick however.

We are all to halt and encamp before we get to the coast and as fast as transportation is ready the troops will be marched aboard at night and push off immediately.

Give my love to all. Fred. is well. Write to me again as soon as you recieve this and direct as usual. Wherever a Mail meets us it will be stoped and we will get our letters.

Adieu but for a short time
ULYSSES

Detroit Michigan
April 27th 1849

My Dearest Julia

I recieved your Telagraphic dispach yesterday morning from which I see that you are on your way to St. Louis. I hope you may find all at home well, and get this soon after your arrival. This you know is my Birth day and I doubt if you will think of it once.—I have a room and am staying at present with Mr. Wallen. Wallen and family are as well as can be expected under present circumstances.

I have rented a neat little house in the same neighborhood with Wallen and Gore[48] In the lower part of the house there is a neat double parlour, a dining room, one small bedroom and kitchen. There is a nice upstares and a garden filled with the best kind of fruit. There is a long arbour grown over with vines that will bear fine grapes in abundance for us and to give away. There are currents and plum & peach trees and infact evrything that the place could want to make it comfortable.

I will have a soldier at work in the garden next week so that by the time you get here evrything will be in the nicest order. I find Detroit very dull as yet but I hope that it will appear better when I get better acquainted and you know dearest without *you* no place, or home, can be very pleasant to me. Now that we are fixed to go to hous keeping I will be after you sooner than we expected when you left. I think about the 1st of June you may look for me. Very likely Ellen will come along and spend the Summer with us.—I hope dearest that you had a very pleasant trip. I know that you have thought of me very often. * * * I have dreamed of you several times since we parted.

[48]Captain John H. Gore (1819–1852) of the 4th Infantry.

I have nothing atal to do here. I have no company and consequently do not go on Guard or to Drills. Mr. Gore and myself are to commence fishing in a day or two and if sucsessful we will spend a great many pleasant hours in that way.

When I commence housekeeping I will probably get a soldier to cook for me, but in the mean time if any good girl offers I will engage her to come when you return.

Dearest I nothing more to write except to tell you how very very dear you are to me and how much I think of you. Give my love to all at home and write to me very soon and often. Yours devotedly

ULYS

P. S. I recieved two letters here for you which I opened and read; the one from Annie Walker I forwarded to you at Bethel.[49] One from Elen I did not send inasmuch as you would be at home so soon. Give my love to Sallie & Annie.

U

Camp Brady
West Point N. Y.
July 13th 1851

My Dearest Julia

I wrote to you last from Quebec on last Sunday. In that letter I gave you a little discription of the place and my travels. From there I returned to Montreal and thence up lake Champlagne.

[49]Bethel, Ohio, in southwestern Ohio, where Grant's parents lived.

My trip has been a very pleasant one and I really felt very glad to get back to the old place where I spent, what then seemed to me, an interminable four years. Evry thing looks as natural as can be, and although I only got here yesterday evry thing seems like home. I should really like very much to be stationed here. Most of the officers are persons who were cadets with me In passing up lake Champlagne the boat stoped for a few minuets at Plattsburg, but I did not see Capt. Wallen or any of the officers stationed there.

I shall leave here to-morrow, probably not to visit the place again—for years. When I get back to Sacket's Harbor I shall remain there until I am ordered away or go to meet you. I suppose I will find a letter at the Harbor from you in which you will say something about when you expect to return. I want to see you and Freddy[50] very much, now particularly, since we are where we can keep house. I will get evrything as comfortable as I can as soon as I go back so that when you come back there will not be much but some little furnature, crockery &c. to get to commence

I occationally see accounts from St. Louis stating that there has been so many deaths, from Cholera, in the city for the last week. These accounts distress me a goodeal. But knowing that you are in the country is a great relief. I hope you and Freddy are quite well. Does the little dog run about yet? I know he must, and try to talk too. I expect he wont know me when he sees me again. His grandma and pa will be sorry to see the little fellow leave them I know, but they wont miss him like I do. By next Summer he will be big enough for me to take him out riding and walking. Who does he like best at his grandpas? I know it is not his aunt Ell. Give my love to all at home dearest Julia and write to me very often. I have but little to write about

[50]Frederick Dent Grant (1850–1912) was born on May 30, 1850.

at present but I will write you a long letter in about one week. I am just as well as it is possible to be. The President that is to be, (I mean Gen. Scott)[51] is here at present. He is looking very well. His wife and daughter are stoping here at the hotel on the Point. The General stops at the hotel about two miles below here. There are a great many visiters here now attending the Cadets parties which take place evry other evening I should like to attend one of them again but I do not know that I can. Next summer if we are still at Sacket's Harbor I will get a leave for a week and bring you here. It is one of the most beautiful places to spend a few days you ever saw. Adieu dear dear Julia, kiss Fred. and all of them at home for me. Come back to me as soon as you think it safe to travel with Fred.

Your affectionate husband
ULYS.

Fort Columbus, Governer's Island N. Y.
June 24th 1852

My Dearest Julia.

It is time now to write my second letter for this week but I must confess that there is but little to write about. I generally go to the city evry day but as I have business with the Quarter Master there I do not get to see much of the city. The other evening I went to see the trained animals you heard me reading about before you left Sackets Harbor. Their performances are truly wonderfull. The monkeys are dressed like men &

[51]Winfield Scott was the unsuccessful Whig candidate for president in 1852.

women, set up and take tea like other persons, with monkeys to wait on the table; they go riding on horseback and in a coach, with dogs for horses, a monkey driving and another acting as footman. During their drive a wheel comes off the carriage and they have an upset. The driver immediately rushes for the dog's heads,—who act as if they were making desperate efforts to run away—and seizes each by the bit and holds them while the footman gets the wheel that come off and brings it to the carriage to be put on again. All this and many other tricks sufficient to fill up an evening they do apparently understanding all the time what they are about. I forgot to say in the begining that I recieved youre note from Cincinnati punctually when due. I was very glad to hear that you had got through without accident to yourself or Fred. and without loss of baggage. Did Clara meet you at the Broadway house?[52] I expect she did not get my letter until you got there. There has been no letter come here for you since you left. I have been expecting a letter from St. Louis, and indeed I am anxious to hear from them before we leave. I shall write to them in the course of a few days. What do they say of your arrangement of spending the summer in Ohio? Dont you think you have taken the wisest course?

It seems now more than probable that we will leave here about the 10th of next month, or as soon after that as transportation can be provided. Maj. Larnard's and Maj. Haller's Companies sail by the way of Cape Horn. It will probably take them from five to six months to go round. I should like the trip by the Horn very much for the sake of seeing all the South American ports that the vessel will necessarily put in too for water &c. Mr. Hunt goes with them for the benefit of his health.—Now as the time approaches for going I am anxious

[52]Clara Rachel Grant (1828–1865), Grant's younger sister; the Broadway Hotel in Cincinnati.

to be off. The later in the season we put off going the worse it will be crossing the Isthmus.

Did you get a letter from Mrs. Gore?[53] She wrote one to you and I want you to be sure and answer it soon. Her brother accompanies her to Calafornia. I think on the whole it is a dangerous experiment for the ladies to go to Calafornia. There is one thing certain they make up their minds before they start to get along with their work without assistance. Some of the ladies of the 2d Infantry who went with their husbands in 1848 have returned and do not intend going back again I believe.

How does little Fred. behave? He has got acquainted well enough I suppose to behave as cuning as he did before he left Sackets Harbor? Does he ever talk about his pa? You must write a greatdeel about the little dog. I want to see him very much. I do not feel as if I can be a great while without seeing you and Fred. I did not know but I would get a leave of absence for a short time and go home but I do not believe it possible. All preparation for starting devolvs on me so that out of all the Regiment I am the only one that cannot get a leave of absence. I am going to Washington next week however, and I may find out something there about the time we will start and if there is time I will go on to Ohio and see you. Adieu my dearest Julia. Give my love to all at home. Kiss Fred. for me. Write soon.

Your affectionate husband
ULYSS.

I forgot to say that I found yours and Freds letter enclosing a lock of each of your hair. I put them away and will take good

[53]Lucy Armistead Morehead Gore (1824–1900).

care of them. I am looking for a letter from you now evry day. Have you rec'd one from St. Louis yet?

U.

Steamer Golden Gate
Near Acapulco, Mexico, Aug. 9th 1852

My Dearest Julia;

I wish I could only know that you, and our dear little ones were as well as I am. Although we have had terrible sickness among the troops, and have lost one hundred persons, counting men, women & children, yet I have enjoyed good health. It has been the province of my place as Quarter Master to be exposed to the weather and climate on the Isthmus, while most of the others were quietly aboard ship, but to that very activity probably may be ascribed my good health. It no doubt will be a relief to you to know that we have been out from Panama over four days and no sickness has broken out aboard. All are healthy and evry minuet brings us towards a better climate.

Among the deaths was that of poor Maj. Gore. The Maj. was taken before daylight in the morning and in the afternoon was dead. Mrs. Gore took his death very hard and then to think too of the trip she had to undergo crossing the Isthmus again! My dearest you never could have crossed the Isthmus at this season, for the first time, let alone the second. The horrors of the road, in the rainy season, are beyond description.—Mrs. Gore will be at home, if she is so fortunate as to stand the trip, before you get this. I hope father and Gennie[54] will go and see her soon. Lieut. Macfeely, 2d Lt. of Maj. Gore's Comp.y, accompanied Mrs. Gore and may go to our house to see you. He promised me that he would. I gave him an order on the Qr. Mr. in New York for $150 00 Mr. Hooker owes me which he gets he will send you.

Mrs. Wallen and the other ladies along are tollerably well, but a goodeal reduced. Mrs. Wallens weight when she got across the Isthmus was 84 lbs. Her children, Harry Nanny & Eddy look quite differently from what they did when they left New York. But thank fortune we are fast approaching a better climate. The Golden Gate takes us nearly 300 miles per day.

We have seen from a Calafornia paper our destination. All but one company goes to Oregon. Head Quarters (and of course me with it) goes to Columbia Barracks, Fort Van Couver, Oregon. In consequence of one company of the Reg.t, and all the sick being left at the Island Flamingo, near Panama, to follow on an other steamer, we will remain at Benecia Cal. for probably a month. Benecia is within a days travels of where John[55] is and of course I shall see him.

You must not give yourself any uneasiness about me now dearest for the time has passed for danger. I know you have borrowed a goodeal of trouble and from the exagerated accounts which the papers will give you could not help it. From Mrs. Gore however you can get the facts which are terrible enough.

I have not given you any discription of any part of our journey, and as I told you in all my letters dearest, I will not until I hear of your being well. I will say however that there is a great accountability some where for the loss which we have

[54]Virginia Paine Grant (1832–1913), Grant's younger sister.
[55]Julia's brother, John Cromwell Dent.

sustained.—Out of the troops at Sackets Harbor some twelve or fifteen are dead, none that you would recollect however except O'Maley, and Sgt. Knox, the one you thought looked so much like Maloney.

Elijah Camp is with us. He goes as sutler, probably with Head Quarters.

Give my love to all at home dearest and kiss our dear little ones for me. Fred, the little dog I know talks quite well by this time. Is he not a great pet? You must not let them spoil him dearest. A thousand kisses for yourself dear Julia. Dont forget to write often and Direct, Hd Qrs. 4th Inf.y Columbia Barracks Fort Van Couver, Oregon.

Adieu dear wife,
Your affectionate husband
ULYS.

P. S. You may be anxious to hear from Maggy.[56] She looks wors than ever. She has been sea-sick ever since she started. She regrets very much that she had not staid with you.

Mrs. Wallen was going to write to you from Panama but Maj. Gore's taking sick prevented.

Again adieu dear dear wife.
U.

[56]Margaret Getz, the wife of an enlisted soldier, worked as a servant for Grant.

Columbia Bks. Fort Vancouver O. T.
December 19th 1852

My Dear Wife;

The Mail Steamer very unexpectedly arrived this morning before I had half my correspondence completed. It brings no Mail however to this point but leaves it at Astoria to be brought up by the river steamer. As the Mail Steamer starts back before we will get the last Mail I cannot tell you whether I will recieve any letters or not; but I am very sure that there are letters for me.

I am, and have been, perfectly well in body since our arrival at Vancouver, but for the last few weeks I have suffered terribly from cramp in my feet and legs, and in one hand. You know I have always been subject to this affliction. I would recover from it entirely in a very short time if I could keep in the house and remain dry. My duties however have kept me out of doors a great deel, and as this is the rainy season I must necessarily suffer from wet and cold. I am now intending to spend one or two weeks indoors, on toast and tea, only going out once per day to see if the supply of wood is kept complete.

This is said by the old inhabitants of Origon to be a most terrible winter; the snow is now some ten inches in depth, and still snowing more, with a strong probability of much more falling. The Thermometer has been from Eigteen to twenty two degrees for several days. Ice has formed in the river to such an extent that it is extremly doubtful whether the Mail Steamer can get back here to take off the Mail by which I have been hoping to send this. You must know the Steamer comes here first, and then goes down the Columbia about four miles, to the mouth of the Willamett river, and up that some fifteen miles to Portland, the largest town in the Territory, though an insignificant little place of but a few hundred inhabitants. I do not know enough of this country to give you the account of it I would like to, having a desire to say nothing that is calculated to mislead others in their opinions of it, but this I can say; so far as I have seen it it opens the richest chances for poor persons who are willing, and able, to work, either in cuting wood, saw logs, raising vegitables, poultry or stock of any kind, of any place I have ever seen. Timber stands close to the banks of the river free for all. Wood is worth five dollars per cord for steamers. The soil produces almost double it does any place I have been before with the finest market in the world for it after it is raised. For instance beef gets fat without feeding and is worth at the door from seventy to one hundred dollars per head, chickens one dollar each, butter one dollar per pound, milk twenty five cents per quart, wheat five dollars a bushel, oats two dollars, onions four dollars, potatoes two dollars and evry thing in the same proportion. You can see from this that mess bills amount to something to speak of. I could not mess alone for less than one hundred dollars per month, but by living as we do, five or six together it does not cost probably much over fifty. * * * I have nearly filled this sheet dear Julia without saying one word about our dear little ones about whom I think so much. If I could see Fred. and hear him talk, and see little Ulys.[57] I could then be contented for a month provided their mother was with them. Learn them to be good boys and to think of their Pa. If your brother does not come out there is no telling when I am to see them and you. It cannot be a great while however because I would prefer sacrifising my commission and try something to continuing this seperation. My hope is to get promotion and then orders to go to washington to settle my accounts. If you, Fred. and Ulys. were only here I would not care to ever go back

[57]Ulysses Simpson Grant (1852–1929) was born on July 22, 1852.

only to visit our friends. Remember me most affectionately to all of them. Kiss Fred. and Ulys. for their Pa and tell them to kiss their ma for me. Maggy and Getz enquire a greatdeel after you and Fred. They evidently think the world and all of him. I hope he is a favorite with his grandpa and all his Uncles and Aunts. I have no dought though the little rascal bothers them enough. When you write to me again dear Julia say a goodeal about Fred. and Ulys. You dont know what pleasure it gave me to read yours and Clara's account of them.

Has Jennie left yet? I suppose so however. How did they like her at your house? Adieu dear dear wife; think of me and dream of me often. I but seldom dream myself but I think of you none the less often.

Your affectionate husband
ULYS. to his dear wife Julia.

Columbia Barracks
Washington Territory
March 31st 1853

My Dearest Wife;

The Mail has just arrived bringing me a very short and very unsatisfactory letter. You speak of not joining me on this coast in a manner that would indicate that you have been reflecting upon a dream which you say you have had until you really imagine that it is true. Do not write so any more dearest. It is hard enough for us to be seperated so far without borrowing immaginary troubles. You know that it was entirely out of the question for you to have come with me at the time I had to come. I am doing all I can to put up a penny not only to enable you and our dear little boys to get here comfortably, but to enable you to be comfortable after you do get here.

You ask why I do not live with the bachilors? I do: that is there are two "messes" and I am in one. Capt.s Brent & Ingalls, Mr. Bomford, Brooke and Eastman are in the same mess that I am. If it is economy you think I should consult all I have to say is that my expenses are about twenty dollars per month less than if I was in the other. We all live and eat in the same house so that Maggy & Getz wash for us and wait upon us; and besides Maggy wastes nothing. The other "mess" is seperated from evry officer so that all expenses of servant hire &c. is surplus.

I am farming now in good earnest. All the ploughing and furrowing I do myself. There are two things that I have found out by working myself. One is that I can do as much, and do it better, than I can hire it done. The other is that by working myself those that are hired do a third more than if left alone.

I was surprised to find that I could run as strait a furrow now as I could fifteen years ago and work all day quite as well. I never worked before with so much pleasure either, because now I feel sure that evry day will bring a large reward.

I believe I told you that I have to do that detestable Quarter Master business this Summer?[58] I dislike it very much. Mr. Camp become very much dissatisfied here and sold out. He was making money much faster than he will ever do again. Notwithstanding his bad luck having his store blown up he has cleared in the few months he has been here more than six thousand dollars, this without two thousand capital to start with.

[58]Grant was attempting to settle his accounts as regimental quartermaster.

Mrs. Wallen is quite well and so are all the officers. Capt. McConnell is here. Mr. Hunt is at Humbolt Bay, Russell at Fort Reading Calafornia. All were well when last heard from. Capt. Wallen met with a serious accident a few days since. He was riding in a wagon and the horse commenced kicking so to save himself he jumped out and fell throughing his right rist entirely out of joint. He will probably be lame in it all Summer.

You can tell your brother that we have had the news all the time that long beards were allowed, at least, on this coast. I have not shaved since I left Calafornia consequently my beard is several inches long. Why did you not tell me more about our dear little boys? I would like to hear some of Fred's sayings. I wish I could have him and his brother here. What does Fred. call Ulys.? What does the S stand for in Ulys.'s name? in mine you know it does not stand for anything! Give my love to all at your house. When you write again dearest write in better spirits.

Does Fred. and his Aunt Ellen get on harmoniously together? I expect she teases him. Cant you have your Dagueriotype taken with Fred. & Ulys. along? if you can send it by Adam's and Co's Express, to Portland, O. T. I presume you have recieved your watch ere this? I have no opportunity of buying any pretty presents here to send you.

Adieu dear dear wife. I shall hope to get a long sweet letter from you next Mail. Kiss our little boys for their pa. A thousand kisses for yourself dear wife.

Your affectionate husband.
ULYS.

☆ ☆ ☆

Columbia Bks. W. T.
July 13th 1853

My Dearest Julia;

It is about 12 o'clock at night, but as the Mail is to leave here early in the morning I must write to-night.—I got your long sweet letter giving an account of our dear little boys at the pic nic where Fred. started behind his Grand ma, but wanted her to ride behinde him before he got through. You know before he could talk he would always persist in having his hands in front of mine when driving. The loose end of the lines never satisfied him.

My dear Julia if you could see the letters they write from my home about our dear little boys it would make you as proud as it does me. I am sure there never was one of my own brothers or sisters who have been more thought of than Fred. & Ulys. In the long letter I got from father he speaks of him as something more than boys of his age. You understand though that I can make allowances for his prejudices either in favor or against; where prejudices are strong predilections are generally right, so I must conclude that Fred. & Ulys. are more than I ever dreamed they were. I dreamed of you last night but not of either of our dear little boys. I mearly saw you for a minuet without having an opportunity of speaking to you and you were gone.

My dear julia I have spoken of speculations so much that the subject is becoming painful, but yet I know you feel interested in what I am doing.—In a former letter I told you, for the first time, of the *downs* of all I had done. (Before I had never met with a *down*.) Since that I have made several hundreds in speculations of various sorts. In groceries which I do not sell, and which are not retailed. I have now a large quantity of pork on hand which is worth to-day ten dollars pr. barrel more than I gave for it at the very place where it was bought. All this will help to buy dresses for Fred. & Ulys. but what interests me most is to know how it is to let their pa see them wear them, and their ma put them on to advantage.

I wrote you that Scott was appointed Inspector General and that it would take me to Fort Reading.—It turns out that he has not been appointed so I must await my place either for Alden's resignation, or for Col. Buchanan's promotion. The first would take me to Fort Jones, of which I have spoken, in former letters: the latter to a detestible place where the mails reach occationally. I should however have command of the post, with double rations and two companies. Wallen is going to San Francisco before you recieve this letter with the intention of seting up a Dairy, Pigery, and market Garden, if practicable. He will go on leave for a few months and then, if sucsessfull, strike out for himself.

You ask how many children Laura has? Before this you know. She has but two; Harry who is a healthy & smart boy, and Nancy who has always, until lately, been heathy.

My dear Julia I have said nothing about the pink leaves upon each of which you say you presed a sweet kiss. I cannot, in this, return the favor on flowers but you may rest assured that I will imprint them when we first meet upon your lips and those of our dear babes.

How can your pa & ma think that they are going to keep Fred. & Ulys always with them? I am growing impatient to see them myself.—Tell Fred. to say *Ugly Aunt Ell* I wont let you learn me anything. * * * so Fred. might say the same to his Uncle. If you cant go your self send him to his other Grandpa's for tuition for a few months.—Indeed dear Julia you must either go with the children or make a very good excuse. Thy want to see you so much. If you have not got means enough I have still some in N. Y. I shall never draw it so long as I remain in this country except in your favor. I hope you got the hundred which I sent you, and also the begining of what Calender was to send you! Give my love to all at your house. I got the pink leaves that you kissed. A thousand kisses for our little boys and yourself.

Adieu dear julia. the Steamer is in sight that is to take this.

Your affectionate husband
ULYS.

Fort Humboldt,
Humboldt Bay, Cal.
February 2d 1854

My Dear Wife.

You do not know how forsaken I feel here! The place is good enough but I have interests at others which I cannot help thinking about day and night; then to it is a long time since I made application for orders to go on to Washington to settle my accounts but not a word in reply do I get. Then I feel again as if I had been separated from you and Fred. long enough and as to Ulys. I have never seen him. He must by this time be talking about as Fred. did when I saw him last. How very much I want to see all of you. I have made up my mind what Ulys. looks like and I am anxious to see if my presentiment is correct. Does he advance rapidly? Tell me a great deel about him and Fred. and Freds pranks with his Grandpa. How does he get along with his Uncle Lewis?

I do nothing here but set in my room and read and occationally take a short ride on one of the public horses. There is game here such as ducks, geese &c. which some of the officers amuse themselves by shooting but I have not entered into the sport. Within eight or ten miles Deer and occationally Elk and black Bear are found. Further back the Grisley Bear are quite numerous. I do not know if I have told you what officers are at this post? Col. Buchanan, Hunt, Collins, Dr. Potts and Lt. Latimer to join. Expected soon. Col. B expects promotion by evry Mail which, if he gets, will bring Montgomery, and leave me in command of the post. Mrs. Collins is the only lady at the post. Dr. Potts however will have his wife here in a short time. The quarters are comfortable frame buildings, backed by a dense forest of immense trees. In front is the Bay. We are on a bluff which gives us one of the most commanding views that can be had from almost any point on the whole Bay. Besides having a view of the Bay itself we can look out to sea as far as the eye can extend. There are four villeges on the Bay. One at the outlet, Humbolt Point is the name, where there are probably not more than 50 inhabitants. What they depend upon for support I do'nt know. They are probably persons who supposed that it would be the point for a City and they would realize a California fortune by the rise of lots. Three miles up the Bay is Bucksport and this garrison Here geting out lumber is the occupation, and as it finds a ready market in San Francisco this is a flourishing little place of about 200. Three miles further up is Euricka with a population of about 500 with the same resourses. The mills in these two villeges have, for the last year, loaded an average of 19 vessels per month with lumber, and as they are building several additional mills they will load a greater number this year. Twelve miles further up, and at the head of the Bay, is Union, the larges and best built town of the whole. From there they pack provisions to the gold mines, and return with the dust. Taking all of these villeges together there are about enough ladies to get up a small sized Ball. There has been several of them this winter.

I got one letter from you since I have been here but it was some three months old. I fear very much that I shall loose some before they get in the regular way of coming. There is no regular mail between here and San Francisco so the only way we have of geting letters off is to give them to some Captain of a vessel to mail them after he gets down. In the same way mails are recieved. This makes it very uncertain as to the time a letter may be on the way. Sometimes, owing to advers winds, vessels are 40 and even 60 days making the passage, while at others they make it in less than two days. So you need not be surprised if sometimes you would be a great while without a letter and then likely enough get three or four at once. I hope the next mail we get to have several from you. Be particular to pay postage on yours for otherwise they may refuse to deliver them at the San Francisco Post Office. I cant pay the postage here having no stamps and not being able to get them. I have sent below however for some.

I must finish by sending a great deel of love to all of you, your Pa. Ma. brother and sisters, niece and nepews. I have not yet fulfilled my promise to Emmy to write her a long letter from Humboldt.

Kiss our little ones for me. A thousand kisses for yourself dear Julia

Your affectionate husband
ULYS

Part II

☆ ☆ ☆

May 1, 1861
to
April 25, 1865

★ ★ ★

GENERAL HEAD QUARTERS—STATE OF ILLINOIS.
ADJUTANT GENERAL'S OFFICE,
SPRINGFIELD, MAY 1st 1861.

Dear Julia;

I have an opportunity of sending a letter direct to Galena[1] by Mr. Corwith and as it will probably reach you a day or two earlyer than if sent by Mail I avail myself of the chance. I enclose also a letter from father for you to read. As I shall probably be home on Saturday evening I shall say nothing about what my intentions are for the future, in fact my plans will have to mature from circumstances as they develop themselvs. At present I am on duty with the Governer,[2] at his request, occupation principally smoking and occationally giving advice as to how an order should be communicated &c. I am going this morning however into the Adjutant General's Office to remain until some regularity is established there, if I can bring about that regularity. The fact is however, as I told the Governer, my bump of order is not largely developed and papers are not my forte and therefore my services may not be as valuable as he anticipates. However I am in to do all I can and will do my best.

We recieve the St. Louis morning papers here at 10 O'Clock a.m. evry day of the day issued and evry day some one is here

[1]Galena, in northwestern Illinois, where Grant had moved with his family in May 1860.

[2]Richard Yates (1818–1873) was the Republican governor of Illinois, 1861–65. Grant briefly served as his military aide.

from the city. The state of affairs there is terrible and no doubt a terrible calamity awaits them. Stationing Ill. Troops within striking distance of St Louis may possibly save the city. Business is entirely prostrated and the best houses are forced to close. I see by the Mo. Republican that Charless Blow & Co are among the number. But for the little piece of stratagem used to get the arms out of the arsenal, to this place, they would have fallen into the hands of the Secessionests and with their hands strengthened with these an attempt would have been made to take the city entirely under controll and terrible slaughter would have taken place. Great numbers of people are leaving Missouri now in evry direction, except South. In some of the Northern towns of the state merchants and business men are leaving with all their personal property. Missouri will be a great state ultimately but she is set back now for years. It will end in more rapid advancement however for she will be left a free state. Negroes are stampeding already and those who do not will be carried further South so that the destiny of the state, in that respect, may now be considered settled by fate and not political parties. Kiss the children for me. You need not write as I will be home so soon

ULYS.

Camp Yates, May 6th 1861

Dear Julia;

There is nothing special to write but you will want to hear often from me during my absence. I too would like to hear from you but so far I have not had the scrape of a pen from you. I presume by Thirsday I shall be on duty in Freeport, mustering in a Regiment there, and if so will be within three hours of Galena and of course will go home. How soon I shall be relieved entirely I do not know. There is no necessity for any volunteers who feel the slightest reluctance about going for already near thirty thousand more have offered their services from this state than can be accepted. There is no doubt but the secessionest contemplated making an attack upon this state but the preperations that have been made here will probably prevent it. We expect here that the next few days will develop a decidedly active policy on the part of the Administration, not perhaps in the way of direct attack, but in stoping all communication with the rebels.

Evrything has been managed most admirably so far in not bringing on a conflict whilst our troops were entirely without drill and totaly unaccustomed to camp life and the proper use of fire arms.—As people from the Southern states are allowed to travel freely through all parts of the North and cannot fail to see the entire unanimity of the people to support the Government, and see their strength in men and means, they must become soon dishartened and lay down their arms. My own opinion is there will be much less bloodshed than is generally anticipated. I believe there will be an attack made on some of the Southern forts and a few decided victories gained when the masses in the south will lay down their arms and the leaders in the rebelion flee to other parts, for their country's good. The worst to be apprehended is from negro revolts. Such would be deeply deplorable and I have no doubt but a Northern army would hasten South to suppress anything of the kind.—Kiss all the children for me. Tell Orvil[3] that when I draw pay here it may be better than our currency, at all events I shall not draw

[3]Orvil Lynch Grant (1835–1881), Grant's younger brother.

anything until I am relieved, and as I did not bring enough with me to pay my board until my return I shall have to draw for from 10 to 20 dollars, depending upon how long I may have to remain. This place, during its present crouded state is more expensive than New York and living abominable.

Love to all

ULYS.

Wish-ton-Wish[4]
May 10th 1861

Dear Julia;

You see by the above that I am writing from your old home. Your father is in the room, absorbed in his paper. Lewis Sheets is fixing a segarita to smoke and Aunt Fanny[5] is seting by me busy with her work. All are well. Soon your father & Lewis Sheets will be left to themselvs at the mercy of Mary[6] and the rest of the darkeys. Aunt Fanny is going back to Ohio and will start in a few days. John is staying at Bill Barnards and only comes out here occationally. I believe he thinks of a colonelcy in the secession army. Your father says he is for the Union but is opposed to having army to sustain it. He would have a secession force march where they please uninterupted and is really

[4]A house on the Dent plantation owned by Julia's brother Lewis Dent.
[5]Probably Frances Dent Gwinn, Julia's aunt.
[6]Mary Robinson, an enslaved woman who worked as a cook. After her emancipation she lived in St. Louis and was interviewed in 1885 following Grant's death.

what I would call a secessionest. Aunt Fanny is strong for the Union and is distressed that your father is not so also. Great numbers of people are leaving St. Louis and Missouri generally. There are two armies now occupying the city, hostile to each other, and I fear there is great danger of a conflict which, if commenced must terminate in great blood shed and destruction of property without advancing the cause of either party.

I called on Mrs. Barrett a few minuets this morning. She and children are well. She says that she will write to you and let you hear from home if you will answer her letters.—Nelly has another little girl. Emma is with her and talks of going up to see you. Your father has given up all notion of going up but I will try and perswade him to change his mind. He is bothered about his June payment to Mitchel: The latter has told him that he must have his money.—I advize to throw the matter into the courts under the Usury laws and stave it off as long as possible.—Sam. Sale is back here and it is said is courting his old wife who has a divorce. His sister-in-law is also back. Miss Enas Pipkins is married to young Poindexter and has gone to California. Jo Pipkins (dont read this out loud) became intimate with a Dutch girl in the neighborhood who was so sensitive to infection as to become a mother without any ceremony from Preacher or Squire. Jo sent her to the city and kept her there for some time but tiring of the seperation he took occation one day, when in the city, to take her some place and have the not tied which made them one, and the heir all right—In the evening he returned bringing his bride with him and the old lady flare up, as you can imagine, and put them both out of the house. All the other neighbors are about as when we left with exception of the changes we have heard of from time to time.

Old Man Rush is still living at White Haven. Does not make enough to pay his rent. White paid $150 00 on his interest. That and the rent of our house in town and the hire of the negroes

I expect helps your father very much. He requires them all. He still has Brooks idyling about. Old Bob, Bon, the Mules Dun colt and now another colt are still roaming at large.

As soon as I get through this letter I am going to leave and will carry the letter with me and mail it. To-morrow I have to be in Belleville. I understand the Regiment to be mustered in there cannot possibly be there so I will have to return again. I have to go back to Mattoon on Monday and on Thursday be at Anna, near Cairo, so that probably it will be about Saturday week before I get back again to Belleville. Once through there and I hope there will be no further need of me. Tell Orvil that he need not be surprised if I should have to draw again for some money, because paying for my meals, and tobacco, (I have not spent a dollar otherwise and have gone without my dinner sometimes to save four bits) takes a goodeal. It will all be made up to me when I start home.

Kiss all the children for me. I think of nothing more that I heard here to write to you.—Aunt Fanny is going to Ohio in company with Jeff Sappington and wife.

Your Husband
U. S.

Since coming into the city I find about 4000. Union troops marching out to the secession encampment to break it up. I very much fear bloodshed.[7]

[7]Union forces captured a secessionist militia encampment outside of St. Louis on May 10, 1861. Rioting broke out as the prisoners were marched through the city, and the Union troops opened fire, killing twenty-eight people.

Naples, Ill.
July 7th 1861

Dear Julia;

We are now laying in camp on the Illinois river spending sunday and will leave to-morrow on our way to Quincy. Up to this time my regiment have made their marches as well as troops ever do and the men have been very orderly. There have been a few men who show a disposition not to respect private property such as hen roosts and gardens, but I have kept such a watch on them, and punished offenders so, that I will venture that the same number of troops never marched through a thickly settled country like this committing fewer depridations. Fred. enjoys it hugely. Our Lieut. Col. was left behind and I am riding his horse so that Fred. has Rondy to ride. The Soldiers and officers call him Colonel and he seems to be quite a favorite.

From Springfield here is one of the most beautiful countries in the world. It is all settled and highly improved. It is all of it the district of the State that sends so much fine stock to St. Louis fair.

Passing through the towns the whole population would turn out to receive us. At Jacksonville, one of the prettyest towns with the most tasty houses that I ever saw, the ladies were all out waving their handkerchiefs, and one of them (I know she must be pretty) made up a boquet and sent me with her name, which by the way the messenger forgot before it come to me. So you see I shall probably never find who the fair donor was.

From present indications we will not remain long at Quincy. There was four regiments ordered there with the expectation of remaining until frost. Two have arrived and been ordered into Missouri. I think my regiment cannot be ordered so soon because we have yet to get all our uniforms & equipments and a part of our arms. It will be at least two weeks before my regt. can be of much service and a month before it can do good service. It was in a terribly disorganized state when I took it but a very great change has taken place. Evry one says so and to me it is very observable. I dont believe there is a more orderly set of troops now in the volunteer service. I have been very strict with them and the men seem to like it. They appreciate that it is all for their own benefit.—Kiss the children for me. Fred. would send his love to all of you but he is out. He says he will answer Susy Felts letter but I am affraid that he will be slow about it.[8] He writes sometimes but never copys letter.

Kisses to you.
ULYS.

Macon City, Mo.
July 19th 1861

Dear Julia;

For the last week I have been kept troting around so that I have neither had time to write nor a place to mail a letter from. I arrived with my Regt. at this place, the junction of the North Missouri road with the Hannibal & St. Jo, about 1 o'clock this afternoon, and will leave to-morrow for Alton unless counter orders should be received in the mean time. For the last two weeks however there has been so little stability

[8]Susan M. Felt (1853–1893) was the daughter of a Galena merchant.

in the orders we receive that I make no calculation one day ahead where I may be. I have now been on the road between here & Quincy, and marching South of the road for nine days. When we first come there was a terrible state of fear existing among the people. They thought that evry horror known in the whole catalogue of disasters following a state of war was going to be their portion at once. But they are now becoming much more reassured. They find that all troops are not the desperate characters they took them for. Some troops have behaved badly in this part of the state and given good grounds for fear but they have behaved no worse than their own people. The Secessionest commit evry outrage upon the Unionests. They seize their property, drive them out of the state &c. and destroy the railroad track wherever they find it without a guard. Yesterday I returned to camp on the line of the R. R. from a little march south as far as the town of Florida. As we went down houses all appeared to be deserted. People of the town, many of them, left on our approach but finding that we behave respectfully and respected private property they returned and before we left nearly evry lady and child visited Camp and no doubt felt as much regret at our departure as they did at our arrival. On our return evry farm house seemed occupied and all the people turned out to greet us. I am fully convinced that if orderly troops could be marched through this country, and none others, it would create a very different state of feeling from what exists now. I have been very well and enjoy myself well. Fred. has told you, no doubt, a long history of his camp. I should like very much to go into Camp some place where you could visit me.

I should like to hear from you and the children oftener. I got one letter from you since I left Springfield and no doubt you have written others. But I am kept so on the wing that they do not reach me. They will all come to hand when I reach Alton.

Give my love to all at Galena. Write all about the children and direct to Alton unless I advise you differently.

ULYS.

Ironton Mo.
August 10th 1861

Dear Julia;

Night before last I come down to Jefferson Bks. with my old Regt. leaving my trunk at the Planter's House flattering myself that at 9 O'Clock the next day I would return to St. Louis, get a leave of absence for a few days and pop down upon you taking you by surprize. But my destination was suddenly changed, 9 O'Clock brought me orders, (and cars to carry a regiment) to proceed at once to this place and assume command. My present command here numbers about 3000 and will be increased to 4000 to-morrow and probably much larger the next day. When I come there was great talk of an attack upon this place and it was represented that there was 8000 rebels within a few miles but I am not ready to credit the report.

I have envited Mr. Rollins of Galena to accept a place on my Staff.[9] I wish you would tell Orvil to say to him that I would like to have him come as soon as possible if he accepts the position.

[9]John A. Rawlins (1831–1869), a lawyer, joined Grant in September 1861 and served as his assistant adjutant general (senior administrative officer) for the remainder of the war.

I sent you some money the other day and requested Ford to write to you.[10] Did he do it? The four gold dollars were thrown in extra for the four children. Bless their hearts I wish I could see them.

I certainly feel very greatful to the people of Ill. for the interest they seem to have taken in me and unasked too. Whilst I was about Springfield I certainly never blew my own trumpet and was not aware that I attracted any attention but it seems from what I have heard from there the people, who were perfect strangers to me up to the commencement of our present unhappy national difficulties, were very unanimous in recommending me for my present position. I shall do my very best not to disappoint them and shall hope by dilligence to render good account of some of the Ill. Vols. All my old Regt. expressed great regret at my leaving them and applied to be attached to my Brigade.

I called to see Harry Boggs the other day as I passed through St. Louis.[11] He cursed and went on like a Madman. Told me that I would never be welcom in his house; that the people of Illinois were a poor misserable set of Black Republicans, Abolition paupers that had to invade their state to get something to eat. Good joke that on something to eat. Harry is such a pittiful insignificant fellow that I could not get mad at him and told him so where upon he set the Army of Flanders far in the shade with his profanity.[12]

Give my love to all the good people of Galena. I hope to be at home a day or two soon but dont you be disappointed if I

[10]Charles W. Ford, a St. Louis lawyer who assisted Grant in business and financial transactions.

[11]Harry Boggs, Julia's cousin, and Grant were partners in a St. Louis real estate firm in 1858–59.

[12]A reference to *Tristram Shandy* (1761–62) by Laurence Sterne (1713–1768): "'Our armies swore terribly in Flanders,' cried my uncle Toby—'But nothing to this.'"

am. Kiss the children for me.—Dont act upon the permission I gave you to go to Covington to board until you hear from me again on the subject.[13]

ULYS.

Cairo, Sept. 20th 1861

Dear Julia,

I believe I have written to you that Dr. Sharp is with me.[14] Casey was also here yesterday and day before.[15] He says Emma was very anxious to come down and see us and probably will be down soon.

I dont know what to say about your coming. I should like to have you here and at the same time I feel that I may have to leave any day. I am in most excelent health, work all the time scarsely ever geting a half hour to take a ride out on horseback.—Evrything looks quiet here now but it may be simply a quiet before a storm.—I believe I have gone longer without writing this time than any time previous since commencing soldiering. Your last letter informed me of poor Simp's death.[16] It did not take me much by surprise but it was right sad that he should die away from home. Did you hear whether he was

[13]Covington, Kentucky, where Grant's parents had moved in 1855.

[14]Dr. Alexander Sharp (1824–1904) had married Ellen Wrenshall Dent in 1854.

[15]James F. Casey (1830–1888) had married Emily (Emma) Marbury Dent on February 14, 1861.

[16]Samuel Simpson Grant (1825–1861), Grant's brother, died on September 13, 1861, near St. Paul, Minnesota.

consious of his approaching end or did he think all the time he would be better again?—In the matter of mourning you can do as you like. I send you $20 00 by express and will send you $100 00 at the end of the month. I want to pay old man Hughlett as fast as possible after which I can supply you liberally enough.[17] I will be able to send $250 00 per month to pay debts and support you and this saving I want to have the best care taken of. I want something after the War, if I am alive, and for you if I am not. How much I should like to see you and the children. It will cost at least $50 00 for you to come down and then you might not be able to stay with me more than one day.

Capt. Rawlins is now with me and Hillyer I have been compelled to give a leave of absence to.[18] His wife is with her mother and her father dying sudden a few days ago, and one of her brothers also, he was obliged to go there to fix up their estate for settlement. He will be back in about ten days.

How did Buck happen to get a whiping?[19] I thought he was too good a boy ever to require anything of the kind. Little Jess must talk now like a book, dont he?[20] Do you think Jess would know me? I wish you would write more about the children, what they say and do. Fred. was a great favorite with the regiment whilst he was with it and I regret now that I did not keep him till this time.

Cairo is not half so unpleasant a place as I supposed it would be. I have a nice office and live with the members of my staff immediately back of it. I did stay about one week at the St. Charles but got very tired of it. Kisses for yourself and

[17]Samuel Hughlett (1808–1864) owned the house Grant rented in Galena.
[18]William S. Hillyer (1831–1874) served as an aide to Grant from September 1861 to May 1863, when he resigned from the army.
[19]Ulysses S. Grant, Jr. (1852–1929), known in his family as "Buck."
[20]Jesse Root Grant (1858–1934).

the children. Love to all our friends. Did Buck kiss Susy Felt for me?

ULYS.

Camp Near Fort Henry, Ten.
Feb.y 5th 1862

Dear Julia,

We returned to-day with most of the remainder of our troops. The sight of our camp fires on either side of the river is beautiful and no doubt inspires the enemy, who is in full view of them, with the idea that we have full 4,000 men. To-morrow will come the tug of war. One side or the other must to-morrow night rest in quiet possession of Fort Henry. What the strength of Fort Henry is I do not know accurately, probably 10,000 men.

To-day our reconnoitering parties had a little skirmishing resulting in one killed & two slightly wounded on our side and one killed and a number wounded on the side of the rebels, and the balance badly frightened and driven into their fortifications.

I am well and in good spirits yet feeling confidance in the success of our enterprise. Probably by the time you receive this you will receive another announcing the result.

I received your letter last night just after I had written to you.

I have just written my order of battle. I hope it will be a report of the battle after it is fought.

Kiss the children for me. Kisses for yourself.

ULYS.

P. S. I was up til 5 o'clock this morning and awoke at 8 so I must try and get rest to-night. It is now 10½ however, and I cannot go to bed for some time yet.

U.

★ ★ ★

Fort Henry, Ten.
Feb.y 6th 1862.

Dear Julia,

Fort Henry is taken and I am not hurt. This is news enough for to-night. I have been writing until my fingers are tired and therefore you must excuse haste and a bad pen. I have written to you every day so far and you cant expect long letters.

Kiss the children for me.

ULYS.

★ ★ ★

Head Quarters, Fort Donelson Ten.
Feb.y 16th 1862

Dear Wife

I am most happy to write you from this very strongly fortified place, now in my possession, after the greatest victory of the season. Some 12 or 15 thousand prisoners have fallen into our possession to say nothing of 5 to 7 thousand that escaped in the darkness of the night last night.

This is the largest capture I believe ever made on the continent.

You warn me against Capt. Kountz.[21] He can do me no harm. He is known as a venimous man whose hand is raised against every man and is without friends or influance. * * * —My impression is that I shall have one hard battle more to fight and will find easy sailing after that. No telling though. This was one of the most desperate affairs fought during this war. Our men were out three terrible cold nights and fighting through the day, without tents. Capt. Hillyer will explain all to you. Kiss the children for me. I will direct my next letter to Covington.

ULYS.

Fort Donelson Ten.
Feb.y 22d 1862

Dear Julia,

You no doubt received a letter from me immediately on your arrival in Covington. I will write to you frequently but short. How long I shall be here is uncertain but not many days I am confidant.

I see from the papers, and also from a dispatch sent me by Mr. Washburn,[22] that the Administration have thought well

[21]Captain William J. Kountz (1817–1904) was the officer in charge of river transportation at Cairo, Illinois. When Grant had him arrested for insubordination in January 1862, Kountz retaliated by charging Grant with public drunkenness. The charges were never acted upon, and Kountz resigned from the army in March 1862.

[22]Elihu B. Washburne (1816–1887) was a Whig, and then Republican, congressman from Illinois, 1853–69. A resident of Galena, Washburne met Grant shortly after the outbreak of the war and became his political patron.

enough of my administration of affairs to make me a Maj. General. Is father afraid yet that I will not be able to sustain myself? He expressed apprehensions on that point when I was made a Brigadier.

There is but little doubt but that Fort Donelson was the hardest fought battle on the Continent. I was extremely lucky to be the Commanding officer. From the accounts received here it must have created a perfect furor through the North.

I am in most perfect health and ready for anything even to chasing Floyd & Pillow.[23] There is but little hope however of ever overhawling them. They are as dead as if they were in their graves for any harm they can do.

To go over the works here it looks as if the enemy had nothing to do but stand in their places to hold them. I have no doubt but you have read of Fort Donelson until you have grown tired of the name so I shall write you no more on the subject. Hope to make a new subject soon. Give my love to all at home. Kiss the children for me and write me all the news.

Tell Mary to write to me also.[24]

ULYS.

Fort Donelson, Feb. 24th 1862.

Dear Julia,

I have just returned from Clarkesville. Yesterday some citizens of Nasville come down there ostensibly to bring surgeons

[23]Confederate generals John B. Floyd (1806–1863) and Gideon J. Pillow (1806–1878) fled Fort Donelson shortly before its surrender.
[24]Mary Frances Grant (1839–1905), Grant's younger sister.

to attend their wounded at that place but in reality no doubt to get assurances that they would not be molested. Johnson with his army of rebels have fallen back about forty miles south from Nashville leaving the river clear to our troops[25] To-day a Division of Gen. Buells Army reported to me for orders.[26] As they were on Steamers I ordered them immediately up to Nashville. "Secesh" is now about on its last legs in Tennessee. I want to push on as rapidly as possible to save hard fighting. These terrible battles are very good things to read about for persons who loose no friends but I am decidedly in favor of having as little of it as possible. The way to avoid it is to push forward as vigorously as possible.

Gen. Halleck is clearly the same way of thinking and with his clear head I think the Congressional Committee for investigating the Conduct of the War will have nothing to enquire about in the West.[27]

I am writing you in great haste a boat being about leaving here. I will write you often to make up for the very short letters I send.

Give my love to all at home and write frequently. Tell me all about the children. I want to see rascal Jess already. Tell Mary she must write to me often. Kiss the children for me and the same for yourself

ULYS.

[25]Confederate General Albert Sidney Johnston (1803–1862).

[26]Union general Don Carlos Buell (1818–1898) commanded the Army of the Ohio, November 1861–October 1862.

[27]Henry W. Halleck (1815–1872) was Grant's immediate superior in the western theater, November 1861–July 1862.

☆ ☆ ☆

Fort Henry March 11th/62

My Dear Julia,

I am just going down to Paducah looking after the interest of the expedition now gone up the Tennessee. Soon more troops will join us then I will go in command of the whole. What you are to look out for I cannot tell you but you may rely upon it that your husband will never disgrace you nor leave a defeated field. We all volunteered to be killed, if needs be, and whilst any of us are living there should be no feeling other than we are so far successful. This is my feeling and believe it is well inculcated among the troops.

My dear Julia I have but little idea from what point I shall next write you. If I knew I would hardly tell but I hope another mark will be made against rebelion.

There is a greatdeel that might be said, in a Military way, but that cannot be properly discussed. If I was ahead of the telegraph however I might say that I believe that I have the whole Tennessee river, to Florance Alabama, safe from any immediate attack. The enemy have preserved one Gunboat, the Dunbar, and may have run her up some creek, during the present high water, to bring out and destroy our transports. That would be my policy yet I do not think it has been adopted. Of course the steamer would be lost but she is lost anyhow and individuals should never take that into account.—We have such an inside track of the enemy that by following up our success we can go anywhere. To counteract us Tennessee at least is trying to bring out all her men. She is doing so so much against the feeling of the men themselvs that within my limited sphere I am giving all the protection possible to prevent forced enlistments. I have written you a military letter when only my love and kisses to the children, and to yourself, was intended. Tell Mary that her last letter was received and she must continue to write. Some day I will find a chance of answering

ULYS.

Savanna, March 29th 1862

Dear Julia,

I am again fully well. I have had the Diaoreah for several weeks and an inclination to Chills & Fever. We are all in *statu qua*. Dont know when we will move. Troops are constantly arriving so that I will soon have a very large army. A big fight may be looked for someplace before a great while which it appears to me will be the last in the West. This is all the time supposing that we will be successful which I never doubt for a single moment.

I heard of your arrival at Louisville several days ago through some Steamboat Capt. and before your letter was received stating that you would start the next day.

All my Staff are now well though most of them have suffered same as myself. Rawlins & myself both being very unwell at the same time made our labors hard upon us. All that were with me at Cairo are with me here, substuting Dr. Brinton for Dr. Simons, and in addition Capt. Hawkins & Capt. Rowley. Rowley has also been very unwell. Capt. Hillyer will probably return home and go to Washington. His position on my Staff is not recognized and he will have to quit or get it recognized.

Capt. Brinck is in the same category. All the slanders you have seen against me originated away from where I was. The only foundation was from the fact that I was ordered to remain at Fort Henry and send the expedition under command of Maj. Gen. Smith.[28] This was ordered because Gen. Halleck received no report from me for near two weeks after the fall of Fort Donelson. The same occured with me I received nothing from him. The consequence was I apparently totally disregarded his orders. The fact was he was ordering me every day to report the condition of my command, I was not receiving the orders but knowing my duties was reporting daily, and when anything occured to make it necessary, two or three times a day. When I was ordered to remain behind it was the cause of much astonishment among the troops of my command and also disappointment. When I was again ordered to join them they showed, I believe, heartfelt joy. Knowing that for some reason I was relieved of the most important part of my command the papers began to surmize the cause, and the Abolition press, the New York Tribune particularly, was willing to hear to no solution not unfavorable to me. Such men as Kountz busyed themselvs very much. I never allowed a word of contridiction to go out from my Head Quarters, thinking this the best course. I know, though I do not like to speak of myself, that Gen. Halleck would regard this army badly off if I was relieved. Not but what there are Generals with it abundantly able to command but because it would leave inexperienced officers senior in rank. You need not fear but what I will come out triumphantly. I am pulling no wires, as political Generals do, to advance myself. I

[28]On March 4, 1862, Halleck relieved Grant of command of the Union expedition up the Tennessee River and replaced him with Brigadier General Charles F. Smith (1807–1862). Halleck soon reversed himself, and on March 17 Grant resumed command of the expedition.

have no future ambition. My object is to carry on my part of this war successfully and I am perfectly willing that others may make all the glory they can out of it.

Give my love to all at home. Kiss the children for me.

ULYS.

Pittsburg, Ten. April 8th 1862

Dear Julia,

Again another terrible battle has occured in which our arms have been victorious. For the number engaged and the tenacity with which both parties held on for two days, during an incessent fire of musketry and artillery, it has no equal on this continent. The best troops of the rebels were engaged to the number of 162 regiments as stated by a deserter from their camp, and their ablest generals.[29] Beaurigard commanded in person aided by A. S. Johnson, Bragg, Breckenridge and hosts of other generals of less note but possibly of quite as much merit. Gen. Johnson was killed and Bragg wounded.[30] The loss on both sides was heavy probably not less than 20,000 killed and wounded altogether.[31] The greatest loss was sustained by the enemy. They suffered immensly by demoralization also

[29]There were seventy-six Confederate regiments at Shiloh.

[30]Albert Sidney Johnston was killed on the afternoon of April 6, 1862. Major General Braxton Bragg (1817–1876), who commanded a corps at Shiloh, was not wounded in the battle.

[31]Shiloh cost the Union 13,000 men killed, wounded, or missing, while Confederate casualties totaled about 10,700.

many of their men leaving the field who will not again be of value on the field.

I got through all safe having but one shot which struck my sword but did not touch me.

I am detaining a steamer to carry this and must cut it short.

Give my love to all at home. Kiss the children for me. The same for yourself.

Good night dear Julia.

ULYS.

Camp in the Field
Near Pittsburg Ten.
April 30th 1862

Dear Julia,

I move from here to-morrow. Before this reaches you probably another battle, and I think the last big one, will have taken place or be near at hand. I mean the last in the Mississippi Valley and this of course implies if we are successful which no doubt we will be. You need give yourself no trouble about newspaper reports. They will all be understood and me come out all right without a single contradiction. Most of all that you have seen has been written by persons who were not here and thos few items collected from persons nominally present, eye witnesses, was from those who disgraced themselvs and now want to draw off public attention. I am very sorry to say a greatdeel originates in jealousy. This is very far from applying however, I think, to our Chief, Halleck, who I look upon as one of the greatest men of the age. You enquire how I was hurt? For several days before the battle of Pittsburg our out Pickets were skirmishing with the enemies advance.[32] I would remain up here all day and go back to Savanna in the evening where I was anxiously looking for the advance of Gen. Buell's column. My object was, if possible, to keep off an attack until Buell arrived otherwise I would have gone out and met the enemy on Friday before they could have got in position to use all their forces advantageously. Friday evening I went back to Savanna as usual and soon after dark a messenger arrived informing that we were attacked. I immediately returned here and started out onto the field on horseback, my staff with me. The night was intensely dark. I soon found that the firing had seased and started to go back to the river. Being very dark and in the woods we had to ride in a slow walk and at that got off the road. In geting back to it my horse's foot either cought or struck something and he fell flat on his side with my leg under him. Being wet and muddy I was not hurt much at the time but being in the saddle all of Sunday and Monday,[33] and in the rain the intervening night without taking off boots or spurs my ancle swelled terribly and kept me on crutches for several days, unable to get on a boot. Col. Riggin is not with me. The rest of the gentlemen are. In addition I have Col. McPherson[34] of the regular Army and one of the nicest gentleman you ever saw, Capt. Reynolds, regular, Lieuts Bowers & Rowley. We are all well and me as sober as a deacon no matter what is said to the contrary. Mrs. Turner & Miss Hadley run on the steamer Memphis carrying sick soldiers to hospital. As I am out from

[32]The battle of Shiloh was initially known in the North as the battle of Pittsburg Landing.

[33]April 6–7, 1862, when the battle of Shiloh was fought.

[34]James B. McPherson (1828–1864) later commanded a corps under Grant and the Army of the Tennessee under William T. Sherman before being killed in the Battle of Atlanta.

the river and they are only here about one day in eight or ten I rarely see them. There are no inhabitants here atall

Kiss all the children for me. Tell Jess I have a five shooter pistol for him. When you hear of me being on the Mississippi river join me leaving all the children except Jess. Draw the hundred dollars you have as a matter of course. If I had an opportunity I would send you $200 00 now. Give my love to all at home. Kisses for yourself.

Good buy
ULYS.

Camp Near Corinth Miss.
May 16th 1862

Dear Julia;

I do hope all suspense about the approaching conflict will be ended before it is time for me to write you another letter. We are moving slowly but in a way to insure success. I feel confidant myself and believe the feeling is general among the troops.

What move next after the attack upon Corinth is hard to predict. It must depend to a great extent upon the movements of the enemy.

Jim Casey is here. He arrived to-day. He is very anxious to have you visit them and says that if you come down he will go with you and Emma to St. Louis on a short visit. I have no objections to the arrangement. They also want Fred. to spend his vacation with them. All were very much pleased with Fred. for his modesty and good sense.—Your father sent Emma a bill of sale for the negroes he gave her. To avoid a possibility of any of them being sold he ought to do the same with all the balance. I would not give anything for you to have any of them as it is not probable we will ever live in a slave state again but would not like to see them sold under the hammer.

Aunt Fanny is back in Mo. She says that Mo. is a better place than she thought it was until she tried Ohio again.

John Dent is going back to the country. Poor John! I pitty him. Dont tell him that I say so though I am anxious to see you and the children once more.

I enjoy most excellent health and am capable of enduring any amount of fatigue. But I want to see this thing over. As I have before said I think the hard fighting in the West will end with the battle of Corinth, supposing all the time that we are successful. Of that, our success, I have no doubt. Kiss all the children for me. I know they are all good and well behaved. Does Jess find any one to fight now that I am away? Give my love to all at home. Write often but dont find fault if you do not receive my letters. I write often enough. Remember me to Mrs. Van Dyke and Mrs. Tweed.

ULYS.

Kiss for yourself

Camp Near Corinth, Miss.
June 3d 1862

Dear Julia,

So confidant was I that I should be starting home by tomorrow or next day, with all my staff, that I let Col. Lagow start last evening with W. W. Smith, your cousin.[35] Necessity however changes my plans, or the public service does, and I must yeald.—In a few weeks I hope to be so stationed that you can join me. Where is hard to say. May be Memphis. I wish Mary would come with you if the latter place should be my destiny and bring all the children to remain until after their vacation. She could then return with the three oldest and let them go to school. As soon as I know definately you will be informed when, where and how to join me. Wm Smith will call to see you on his way to Washington Pa and will deliver Jess' pistol. Tell Jess he must hurt nobody with it but all the little boys may look at it.

I will move up to-morrow into Corinth Corinth is a new town of but about three years growth, neatly built and probably contained about 1500 inhabitants. Now it is desolate the families all having fled long before we got possission, windows broken furniture broken and destroyed, and no doubt the former occupants destitute and among friends but little better off than themselvs. Soldiers who fight battles do not experience half their horrors. All the hardships come upon the weak, I cannot say innofensive, women and children. I believe these latter are wors rebels than the soldiers who fight against us. The latter mostly are heartily tired of the war. This is the evidence of prisoners and deserters who come in at least.

It is now pretty certain that we will take near 10.000 prisoners, 20,000 stand of arms and now doubt a greater number of men have deserted and will be lost to the rebel army than the whole number taken.

Give my love to all at home. Kiss the children for me and accept the same to yourself.

ULYS.

[35]Clark B. Lagow (1828–1867) served as an aide to Grant from August 1861 to November 1863; William Wrenshall Smith (1830–1904), a merchant and banker from Pennsylvania.

Corinth Mississippi,
June 9th 1862

My Dear Julia,

I expected by this time to be at home, but fate is against it.—You need not now look for me atal but you may look for a letter soon where to join me. I do not know where myself but in all probability it will be in West Tennessee.

Privately I say to you that when I talked of going home and leaving my command here there was quite a feeling among the troops, at least so epressed by Gen. officers below me, against my going. I will have to stay. It is bearly possible that I may be able to leave long enough to go after you and bring you on. If so I will do it.—It would afford me the greatest pleasure to be relieved from active duty for even a short time. People in civil life have no idea of the immense labor devolving on a commander in the field. If they had they never would envy them. Rawlins has become so perfectly posted in the duties of the office that I am relieved entirely from the routine. Cols. Hillyer & Lagow are also familiar with the duties and Aid me out of doors materially.

Although Gen. Sherman has been made a Maj. Gen. by the battle of Shiloh I have never done half justice by him. With green troops he was my standby during that trying day of Sunday, (there has been nothing like it on this continent, nor in history.) He kept his Division in place all day, and aided materially in keeping those to his right and left in place—He saw me frequently and received, and obeyed, my directions during that day, but some others, I will say only one other, may have forgotten them. In writing this last sentence it would leave an inference against a commander on Sunday. I would imply nothing of the sort, but against one of my commanders on Monday.[36]

Give my love to all at home. Kiss the children for me and accept the same for your self. Has Jess got his pistol yet.—I sent it by Wm Smith.

Goodbuy
ULYS.

Corinth Miss.
June 12th 1862

Dear Julia

It is bright and early (before the morning mail leaves) and I thought to write you that in a few days, Monday the 16th probably, I would leave here. I hope to be off on Monday for Memphis and if so want you to join me there. I will write again however just before starting and it may be will have arranged to go after you instead of you coming by yourself.—I would love most dearly to get away from care for a week or two.

I am very well. This is apparently an exceedingly fine climate and one to enjoy health in.—Citizens are begining to return to Corinth and seem to think the Yankees a much less bloody, revengeful and to be dreaded people, than they had been led to think.

In my mind there is no question but that this war could be ended at once if the whole Southern people could express their unbiased feeling untramelled by leaders. The feeling is

[36]Probably a reference to Brigadier General Alexander M. McCook (1831–1903), who commanded a division in the Army of the Ohio at Shiloh.

kept up however by crying out Abolitionest against us and this is unfortunately sustained by the acts of a very few among us.—There has been instances of negro stealing, persons going to the houses of farmers who have remained at home, being inclined to Union sentiments, and before their eyes perswaid their blacks to mount up behind them and go off. Of course I can trace such conduct to no individual but believe the guilty parties have never heard the whistle of a single bullet nor intentionally never will.

Give my love to all at home. Kisses for yourself and children.

Your husband
ULYS.

Oxford Miss.
Dec. 13th 1862

Dear Julia,

Bowers is here just returning and I take advantage of the occation to write you a few lines. I did intend moving Hd Quarters south to Springdale to-day but as it looks so much like rain and there is no special necessity for it I will not move until Monday or Teusday next. I have had no letter from home since we left Lagrange nor no letter for you, from any quarter, except one from Ford enclosed in one to me. The bottle of Bourbon sent by Mrs. Davies I sent over to Gen. Sherman. Myself nor no one connected with the Staff ever tasted it.

Kiss Jess for me. Remember me to Lagow.

ULYS.

Near Vicksburg
Feb.y 11th 1863.

Dear Julia,

This evening I leave here to go up to Lake Providence to superintend matters there for a few days. We are not much nearer an attack on Vicksburg now apparently than when I first come down, but still as the attack will be made and time is passing we are necessarily coming nearer the great conflict. I have been remarkably well since leaving Memphis. I now feel about as I did on leaving Memphis last summer.

I met with a great loss this morning. Last night, contrary to my usual habit, I took out my teeth and put them in the wash bason and covered them with water. This morning the servant who attends to my stateroom, blacks my boots &c, come in about daylight and finding water in the bason threw it out into the river teeth and all. I wrote to Dr. Hamline by the same Mail that takes this to bring with him if he should come down here material to take an impression and make me a new sett. If the Dr. is in Memphis I wish you would get one of the officers to hunt him up and tell him of my misfortune.

The river is now so high that the most of this country would be under water if the levees were cut.

Kisses for yourself and Jess. Tell Jess he must be a good boy and learn his lessons. If he learns all his letters before I see him again I will give him something pretty.

Goodbuy

ULYS.

Before Vicksburg Miss
Feb.y 14th 1863.

Dear Julia,

I have written two or three letters in the last two days and therefore have but little to add now. One thing however was suggested by the letter you forwarded to me from home that I forgot to mention in my letter to you. They say that $82 00 has been received for the children and you speak of sending more by express. Do you not remember that I put fifty-two dollars in a letter that was to have been taken by Col. Carpenter? What ever became of that? I am remarkably well. Hope in the course of ten days more to be making a move. My confidance in taking Vicksburg is not unshaken unless if our own people at home will give their moral support. At present however they are behaving scandalously. A soldier now geting home to Illinois, Indiana or Ohio there is no way of geting him back. Northern secessionest defend and protect them in their desertion. I want to see the Administration commence a war upon these people. They should suppress the disloyal press and confine during the war the noisy and most influential of the advocates.

Kiss the children for me. The same for yourself. I will address my next letter to Covington.

ULYS.

Millikin's Bend La.
April 20th 1863.

Dear Julia,

I want you to go to St. Louis and stay there until you get the deed from your brother John for the 60 acres of land *where our house* is,[37] and have it recorded. Also get the deed for 40 acres where your brother Lew's. house is and have it recorded. Be shure and have this done right. Then lease out the farm to some good and prompt tenant, for five years, giving them the privilege of taking off every stick of timber and puting the whole place in cultivation. Bind them to take care of the house, fences and fruit trees. Place Bass Sappington or Pardee in charge to collect the rent and when all is done say to your father that the house is for his use as long as he wants it and the rents are to go to him for the other place.

If John Dent wants to go to Calafornia you may offer him $1600 for 40 acres adjoining the 60 acres. If he desires this have this deed recorded also before you leave. I want it distinctly understood however that I do not desire this trade and only make the offer to enable him to go and look after other property he has. If it was not that I am poor and have not a dollar except my savings in the last two years I would not hesitate to furnish him all the necessary money without any other guarantee than the conciousnous that I had done him a favor.

In case you make this trade it will be necessary for you to go to Galena to get the money. You can explain to Orvil that I have purchased property and paid $3000 on it and have to pay $1600 more. You can settle the difference they make out against me at the store but try and have Lank. who kept the

[37]Hardscrabble, the house Grant built on the Dent plantation in 1856.

books, to make up the account. Ask Orvil how brother Simps estate was settled. Inform him that I should never have mentioned it in the world but some of them are seting so much higher merit upon money than any other earthly consideration that I feel it a duty to protect myself. If you go to Galena be patient and even tempered. Do not expose yourself to any misconstruction from a hasty remark. Be firm however. Give up no notes except what you get cashed unless they pay the whole with the interest accrued. In that case you can allow them for what they say I owe with the same interest upon the debt they pay you. Should you however get but a part of the money give only the notes they pay. Tell Orvil that on final settlement I will allow the same interest that I receive. So long as they hold money of mine they need not be afraid to trust me.

This business all settled you can visit any of your friends until you hear that I am in Vicksburg when you can join me as soon as possible. Try and engage a Governess to teach the children, one who speaks German if possible. Do not make a possitive bargain however until you write to me.

U. S. GRANT

Grand Gulf Miss.
May 3d 1863,

Dear Julia,

I have just got in here after a battle fought and won by us. I have been on horseback since early this morning, rode in here leaving my army fifteen miles in the country, have written dispatches and a report for Washington and have to go back tonight. This will keep me up until 12 o'clock tonight. Fred is very well, enjoying himself hugely. He has heard balls whistle and is not moved in the slightest by it. He was very anxious to run the blockade of Grand Gulf. My victory at this place, over Bowen, is a most important one. Management I think has saved us an imense loss of life and gained all the results of a hard fight. I feel proud of the Army at my command. They have marched day and night, without tents and with irregular rations without a murmer of complaints. I write in very great haste. Mr. Washburn is here with me. He is immensly delighted as is also Gov. Yates. Jim Casey is here but I have had no opportunity of talking to him yet.

Good buy dear Julia,
ULYS.

Walnut Hills, Miss.
June 15th 1863.

Dear Julia,

When I last wrote I told you that you might come down. I thought then I would write no more expecting that you would leave before another letter would reach you. But you may remain long enough to get another letter. If you should come down before Vicksburg falls you would hardly see me until the place is taken however. My Hd Qrs. are six miles from the landing with the road always blocked with wagons bringing supplies for our immense army. My duties are such that I can scarsely leave.—I have continued well except an attack of Dysentery which now has entirely left me. Fred. has been complaining a little for a few days. His Uncle Lewis was down this morning and I let him go back with him to spend a short time. I have proposed to Fred. to go to St. Louis several times but he objects. He wants to see the end of Vicksburg. Everything looks highly favorable here now. I have the town closely invested and our Rifle Pitts up so close to the enemy that they cannot show their heads without being shot at at short enough range to kill a squirrel. They dare not show a single gun on the whole line of their works. By throwing shells every few minuets the people are kept continuously in their caves. They must give out soon even if their provisions do not give out. Some of the rebels are escaping to our lines every night. They all unite in discribing every thing inside as in a deplorable condition. Troops are on less than half rations and many poor people without anything. I decline allowing any of them to come out.

I want to see you and the children very much. Miss[38] and Jess I know will be delighted with their pony. He is so small that Fred can ride him with one foot draging on the ground. You must not neglect bringing a little saddle for both Jess & Miss, and a small bridle. I sent up to Memphis and got all the clothing I wanted except cravats. You may bring me two black ones and half a dozen light ones.—I paid Lewis the $500 still due on Wish ton Wish. No one on my staff has resigned except Hillyer and he remained one month after the acceptance of his resignation. Lagow has gone home sick and I expect never to recover. He may get up so as to return but will never be well. All my staff are well. Why did you not stop and see Nelly on your way down?

Remember me to all. Kisses for yourself and children.

ULYS.

[38]Ellen (Nellie) Wrenshall Grant (1855–1922), their daughter.

☆ ☆ ☆

June 29th 1863

Dear Julia,

During the present week I think the fate of Vicksburg will be decided. Johnston is still hovering beyond the Black river and will attack before you receive this or never.[39] After accumulating so large an army as he has, at such risk of loosing other points in the Confederacy by doing it, he cannot back out without giving battle or loosing prestige. I expect a fight by Wednsday or Thursday. There may be much loss of life but I feel but little doubt as to the result.—Saturday or Sunday next I set for the fall of Vicksburg.[40] You can come down then and bring the children with you. We will have to make some arrangement for them to go to school as soon as schools open after vacation. You will have to stay with them as a general thing but by selecting a good place for you and them to board you can visit me a part of the time, when I am still. I do not expect to be still much however whilst the war lasts.

Fred. has returned from his uncles. He does not look very well but is not willing to go back until Vicksburg falls. I think I will send him a trip as far North as St. Paul after the fall of Vicksburg. Remember me to all at home. You do not say whether you have leased the farm or not. I do not want White to hold it.

Kiss the children for me.

ULYS.

[39]Confederate General Joseph E. Johnston (1807–1891).
[40]The Vicksburg garrison surrendered on Saturday, July 4, 1863.

Chattanooga Tennessee
October 27th 1863.

Dear Julia,

The very hard ride over here and necessary exercise since to gain a full knowledge of location instead of making my injury worse has almost entirely cured me.[41] I now walk without the use of a crutch or cane and mount my horse from the ground without difficulty. This is one of the wildest places you ever saw and without the use of rail-roads one of the most out-of-the way places. To give you an idea of its inaccessibility I have only to state that the waggons with our baggage left Bridgeport, the present rail-road turminus, fifty miles distant by the road they have to travel, on the 23d inst. It is now 10 O'Clock at night of the 27th and they have not yet arrived and I hardly expect them to-morrow. Then too six-mule teams are not loaded with what two would easily pull on ordinary dirt roads. We have not consequently been able to start Messes.—Ross remained back at Nashville to lay in supplies but as he has not yet come up to Bridgeport I suspect he has had to go, or send, to Louisville for them. When they will get up is hard to surmise. I am making a desperate effort however to get possession of the river from here to Bridgeport and if I do it will facilitate bringing supplies very much.[42]

[41]Grant injured his left leg when his horse fell on him during a visit to New Orleans on September 4, 1863.
[42]Chattanooga had been under siege since the Confederate victory at Chickamauga on September 20, 1863. The siege was broken on October 30.

There are but very few people here and those few will have to leave soon. People about Vicksburg have not seen War yet, or at least not the suffering brought on by war.

I have received no line from you yet. I feel very anxious to hear from the children. Tell Fred and Buck they must write at least one letter each week to you or me.

Kisses for yourself and Jess.

ULYS.

When do you think of starting on your trip to Ohio? You ought to start soon or you will not be able to go this Fall.

U.

Chattanooga Tennessee,
November 2d 1863,

Dear Julia,

I have received your second letter stating that you had not yet heard from me. Dr. Kittoe wrote to you the next day after our arrival and I wrote the same or next day. Since that I have written several times. You still ask to come to Nashville! I do not know what in the world you will do there. There is not a respectable hotel and I leave no one of my Staff there. You would be entirely among strangers and at an expensive and disagreeable place to live. Bowers is there now, but is there only to close up unfinished business and to pack up and dispose of papers useless to carry into the field. This is just as unsuitable a place for you to be as Millikins Bend.[43] More so for there you could get by Steamer and here you cannot.

I see the papers again team with all sorts of rumors of the reason for recent changes. This time however I do not see myself abused. I do not know whether this is a good omen or not. I have been so accustomed to seeing at least a portion of the press against me that I rather feel lost when not attacked from some quarter. The best of feeling seems to prevail with the Army here since the change. Thomas has the confidance of all the troops of Rosecrans late command. The consolidation of the three Departments into one command also seems to give general satisfaction.[44]

I hope you have had a pleasant visit to Ohio. If I had thought of it I would have advised you to have asked Alice Tweed to have accompanied you. I hope you saw father & mother as you passed through Cincinnati? I would not have asked you to cross the river to see them. I know mother will feel very badly if she does not get to see you & Jess. Kiss the little rascal for me. Tell him to be a good boy and learn his lessons so that he can write letters to me. Kisses for yourself dear Julia.

ULYS.

[43]Milliken's Bend, Louisiana, near Vicksburg.

[44]On October 18, 1863, Grant became commander of the new Military Division of the Mississippi, with authority over the Departments of the Ohio, Tennessee, and Cumberland. Grant then replaced William S. Rosecrans (1819–1898) with George H. Thomas (1816–1870) as commander of the Army of the Cumberland.

Chattanooga November 30th/63

Dear Julia,

The fighting at this place, as you will know before you receive this, is all over at Chattanooga.[45] I went with the advance, in pursuit over twenty miles. Every mudhole for that distance showed evidence of the utter route and demoralization of the enemy. Wagons, & Caissons would be found stuck in the mud and abandoned in the haste of the enemy to get away. Small arms were found every where strewn. We have now forty-two pieces of Artillery taken from the enemy and over six thousand stand of small arms and no doubt many more will be found. The number of prisoners taken is about seven thousand.

Your letter speaking of Col. Pride being with me is received. How did you hear he was with me? He is not nor have I any intention of ever having him at Head Quarters again. There is a rail-road to be put in running order from Nashville to Decatur which I wanted him to superintend the building of but I do not suppose he will do it. The job would be simply to superintend workmen whilst they were building bridges and when that is done he would be relieved. Tell me how he has offended you?

I shall not probably remain in Chattanooga many weeks longer. Where I expect to go would not be proper for me to state, but I have no expectation of spending a winter in idleness.

I will send with this some of the Photographs taken here, also photographs of two General officers that you have not yet got, and one of Deshon, a classmate of mine who is now a

[45]The battle of Chattanooga, November 23–25, 1863, ended in a decisive Union victory.

Catholic priest.[46] Remember me to your Uncle & his family. Kisses for you and Jess.

ULYS.

Culpepper C. H. Va
March 25th 1864

Dear Julia,

I arrived here yesterday well but as on my former trip brought wet and bad weather. I have not been out of the house today and from appearances shall not be able to go out for several days. At present however I shall find enough to do in doors. From indications I would judge the best of feelings animate all the troops here towards the changes that have been made.—I find mails follow me up with remarkable promptitude. More letters reach me than I can answer.—I hope you have entirely recovered? It is poor enjoyment confined to bed in Washington.—There is one thing I learned in Washington just on leaving that wants attending to. You know breakfast lasts from early in the morning until about noon, and dinner from that time until night. Jess runs about the house loose and seeing the guests at meals thinks each time it is a new meal and that he must necessarily eat. In this way he eats five or six times each day and dips largely into deserts. If not looked after he will make himself sick.—Have you heard from Fred.? No

[46]George Deshon (1823–1904) graduated from West Point in 1843, resigned from the army in 1851, and became a priest in 1855.

doubt he got home safely. I shall go down to Washington on Sunday. You need not mention it however.—I have sent in my recommendations for staff appointments placing Fred's name among them. I will know by to-morrow if they are approved. No doubt they will be however. I have put in the name of Capt. H. Porter, a very valuable regular officer, about such as Comstock, and still left one vacancy so that if Wilson should fail in his confirmation I can appoint him.[47] I do not apprehend however any danger of his confirmation.

Kisses for yourself & Jess.

ULYS.

Culpepper Apl. 17th 1864

Dear Julia,

Bowers will leave here on Tuesday, (Washington on Wednesday) for the West. If your mind is made up to accompany him telegraph me and I will go in to see you off. I dislike however very much going in again. In the first place I do not like being seen so much about Washington. In the second it is not altogether safe. I cannot move without it being known all over the country, and to the enemy who are hovering within a few miles of the rail-road all the time. I do not know that the enemy's attack on the road last Friday was with the view of ketching

[47]Julia's brother Frederick. T. Dent, Horace Porter (1837–1921), and Cyrus D. Comstock (1831–1910) served as aides to Grant in the 1864–65 campaign. James H. Wilson (1837–1925) was awaiting Senate confirmation as a brigadier general of volunteers.

me, but it was well timed. If you intend going either get Mr. Stanton or Mr. Chadwick to telegraph me.[48]

I understand Jess has been having a fight in the hall! How is that?—Fred has said nothing about Helen coming East.[49] He told me that when you went out she would have to leave your fathers. Kisses for yourself and Jess. Gen. Hunter will deliver this and tell you how we are living. Plain and well, surrounded with mud. I do not say you must go but I see no particular reason for your remaining longer. I shall certainly go to Washington but once more and that will be to see you off. As soon as it is possible for me to settle I will send for you and the children. Should we be so fortunate as to whip the enemy well, I feel that after that there will be no campaigning that I cannot direct from some one place.

Kisses again.

ULYS.

Culpepper April 24th/64

Dear Julia,

I see by the papers you are having a good time in New York. Hope you will enjoy it. But don't forget Jess and loose him in the streets in all the excitement, New York is a big place and you might not find him.—A telegraph dispatch announces

[48]Secretary of War Edwin M. Stanton (1814–1869); Chadwick was probably one of the proprietors of the Willard Hotel in Washington, D.C.
[49]Helen Louise Lynde Dent (1836–1922), the wife of Frederick T. Dent.

that the sword has been voted to me![50] I am rather sorry for it, or rather regret that my name has been mixed up in such a contest. I could not help it however and therefore have nothing to blame myself for in the matter.

The weather has been very fine here for a few days and dried the roads up so as to make them quite passable. It has commenced raining again however, and is now raining so hard, that it will take a week to bring them back to what they were this afternoon.

Remember me kindly to Col. and Mrs. Hillyer and the children. Kisses for yourself and Jess. I rather expected a letter from you this evening, but none came. I will write to the children tomorrow evening. Don't forget to send me any letters you receive from them. I know they must be anxious to see you back.

ULYS.

Culpepper May 2d 1864

Dear Julia,

The train that takes this letter will be the last going to Washington. This then is the last letter you can receive from me until the Army strikes some new base. The telegraph will be working for a few days however so that you will hear through the papers what the Army is doing.

[50]At the recent Sanitary Fair in New York City each donor of a dollar was entitled to vote for either Grant or George B. McClellan to receive a ceremonial sword. By the close of the Fair on April 23, 1864, Grant had received 30,291 votes, McClellan 14,509.

Before you receive this I will be away from Culpepper and the Army will be in motion. I know the greatest anxiety is now felt in the North for the sucsess of this move, and that the anxiety will increase when it is once known that the Army is in motion. I feel well myself. Do not know that this is any criterion to judge results because I have never felt otherwise. I believe it has never been my misfortune to be placed where I lost my presence of mind, unless indeed it has been when thrown in strange company, particularly of ladies. Under such circumstances I know I must appear like a fool.

I received a letter from Buck this evening. It was very well written. He says he can speak German a little.

All your letters reach me the second day after they are written. If I do not get one to-morrow I shall not expect to hear from you for several weeks. All the letters you write however send to me directed to Washington and they will come to me by first opportunity.

Love and Kisses for you and Jess.

ULYS.

Near Spotsylvania C. H. Va.
May 13th 1864

Dear Julia,

The ninth day of battle is just closing with victory so far on our side. But the enemy are fighting with great desperation entrenching themselves in every position they take up. We have lost many thousand men killed and wounded and the enemy have no doubt lost more. We have taken about eight thousand prisoners and lost likely three thousand. Among our wounded the great majority are but slightly hurt but most of them will be unfit for service in this battle. I have reinforcements now coming up which will greatly encourage our men and discourage the enemy correspondingly.

I am very well and full of hope. I see from the papers the country is also hopeful.

Remember me to your father and Aunt Fanny. Kisses for yourself and the children. The world has never seen so bloody or so protracted a battle as the one being fought and I hope never will again. The enemy were really whipped yesterday but their situation is desperate beyond anything heretofore known. To loose this battle they loose their cause. As bad as it is they have fought for it with a gallantry worthy of a better.

ULYS.

June 1st 1864

Dear Julia,

There has been a very severe battle this afternoon and as I write, now 9 O'clock at night firing is still continued on some parts of the battle line.[51] What the result of the days fighting has been I will know but little about before midnight and possibly not then. The rebels are making a desperate fight

[51]An attack by Union troops on the Confederate lines at Cold Harbor, Virginia, was repulsed on June 1, 1864.

and I presume will continue to do so as long as they can get a respectable number of men to stand.

I send pay accounts for May to Washington by Col. Bowers, who starts in the morning, with directions to send you $800 00 of it. April pay I sent all to Jones in liquidation of my indebtedness. In June I hope to pay all up.—I see by the papers dear little Nellie acquitted herself very handsomely at the Sanitary Fair. I would like very much to see you and the children but cannot hope to do so until this Campaign is over. How long it will last is a problem. I can hardly hope to get through this month.—With the night booming of Artillery and musketry I do not feel much like writing so you must excuse a short letter this time. Dr. Sharp is with me apparently enjoying himself very much. Fred. has been suffering intensely for several days with rheumatism. He has to lay upon his back in the ambulance unable to turn himself. I think he will be well in a day or two. Orvil Grant is at the White House[52] and will probably be here to morrow.

My love to all. Kisses for yourself and the children.

ULYS.

June 7th/64

Dear Julia,

I wrote to you last night but having had my hair cut to-day and remembering that you asked me to send you a lock I now

[52]White House, Virginia, on the Pamunkey River.

write again to send it. I have nothing to add. To-day has been the quietest since leaving Culpepper. There has been no fighting except a little Artillery firing and some skirmishing driving the enemy's pickets south of the Chickahominy at two of the bridges below our main line. War will get to be so common with me if this thing continues much longer that I will not be able to sleep after a while unless there is an occational gun shot near me during the night.

Love and kisses for you and the children.

ULYS.

City Point Va. June 15th/64

Dear Julia,

Since Sunday we have been engaged in one of the most perilous movements ever executed by a large army, that of withdrawing from the front of an enemy and moving past his flank crossing two rivers over which the enemy has bridges and rail-roads whilst we have bridges to improvise. So far it has been eminently successful and I hope will prove so to the end. About one half my troops are now on the South side of James River. A few days now will enable me to form a judgement of the work before me. It will be hard and may be tedious however.

I am in excellent health and feel no doubt about holding the enemy in much greater alarm than I ever felt in my life. They are now on a strain that no people ever endured for any great length of time. As soon as I get a little settled I will write Buck and Missy. each a letter in answer to theirs and will write to

Cousin Louisa[53] who I have received another short letter from enclosing Buck's. I want the children to write to me often. It improves them very much. I forgot that I had received a letter from Fred. since I wrote to him. I will answer his first.

Give my love to all at home. Did you receive the draft for $800 00? It is all I can send you until the end of July.—Kisses for you and the children.

ULYS.

City Point Va. June 19th 1864

Dear Julia,

I send you three steoriscopic views taken at Mattaponix Church, near Spotsylvania Court House.[54] Brady is along with the Army and is taking a great many views and will send you a copy of each. To see them you will want a Sterioscope. Send to Covington for Buck's or buy one.

I received a letter from you just after I had mailed one and now forget the questions you asked.—I received two copies of Miss. Photograph

There has been some very hard fighting here the last four days, but now I hope it is over.

[53]Louisa Boggs (1824–1917), the wife of Julia's cousin Harry Boggs.

[54]The photographs, taken on May 21, 1864, show Grant and George G. Meade (1815–1872), the commander of the Army of the Potomac, holding a council of war while seated on wooden pews outside the Massaponix Church. They were taken by Timothy O'Sullivan (1840–1882), a photographer employed by Mathew Brady.

There are no buildings here to live in and no place for you and the children to stay or I might send for you. I will however send down to Fortress Monroe and if a suitable place can be found there for you you and the children may spend their vacation there where I can see you occationally. If you do come wont Cousin Louisa come with you? I will ascertain about this as soon as possible.

Did I tell you that my horse rail-road stock paid 5 per cent the last quarter? This makes that $5.000 investment pay over $100 00 per month.

Love and kisses for you and the children and love to Aunt Fanny and your father.

ULYS.

City Point, Va. July 7th 1864.

Dear Julia,

I received two letters from you this evening, written after you had received mine stating that you could come to Fortress Monroe to spend the Summer. I am satisfied it is best you should not come. It would be expensive to furnish a house there and difficult supplying it afterwards. The camp life we are leading you would not be able to be where I am often and then only to come up and go immediately back, with an express boat that might be running at the time.

I wrote to you in my last why not make the same arrangement for the children as last year? Permanency is a great thing for children at school and you could not have a better home for them than with Louisa Boggs. If they were with her I should always feel easy for you to leave them for two or three months to stay with me if I was where you could possibly be with me. I want the children to prossecute their studies, and especially in languages. Speaking languages is a much greater accomplishment than the little parapharnalias of society such as music, dancing &c. I would have no objection to music being added to Nellies studies but with the boys I would never have it occupy one day of their time, or thought.

If you think it advisable to go some place where you can keep the children with you, and where they will be at a good school, I will not object. But I cannot settle for you where such a place would be, probably the City of St. Louis would be as good as any other, for the present. Love and Kisses for yourself and the children. How much I wish I could see you all.

ULYS.

City Point, Va, Aug 1st 1864.

Dear Julia,

Since writing to you before about going to Princeton N. J. I have made further enquiries. I find they have as fine schools there as is to be found in the country. It is one of the nicest places to live, the best society, and near to every place in the East. It is close to Long Branch, a favorite Summer resort, near to New York, near Philadelphia, within seven or eight hours of Washington City and within a day, nearly, of here. If you leave for me to decide I say emphatically you will go to Princeton. As soon as I have your say in this matter I will send Col. Porter of my Staff (he was sent to Princeton to school before he went to West Point) to secure you a house. I will leave it to you whether to keep house or board. In my opinion it will be better, if you go there, to keep house. By having a good trusty house keeper you can all ways leave home for a few days and whilst in the East I can always get home, if not in a few hours, in a day at furthest. You would bring Little Rebel with you for the children to ride and I would send you Egyt for you to drive. I know with these, and Jess to *escort*, you would be happy. I could not send you the black pony Jeff Davis. He has got to be one of the most beautiful horses you ever saw, very fleet, and he always was just as easy as a rocking chair. I have been offered $1.000 for him and $1.200 for the horse given to me by Mr. Grant of Cincinnati. Of course I could not sell them but it shows how fine they are regarded.

Love to all and kisses for you and the children. I write, as usual, after every body else is in bed, and with full twelve hours constant wrighting to do, which I must do, before me. Tell Dr Barrett I rec'd his letter this evening. He must not be disappointed if I do not answer him.

ULYS.

City Point Va. Sept. 14th 1864.

Dear Julia,

Your letter speaking of the new embarassment which has arisen in not being able to send the boys to College without having them board away from home has just reached me. As school does not commence until the begining of next month it will not be necessary for me to write to the principle about it as I shall try to slip up there for a day and see him in person. As to Jess refusing to go to school I think you will have to show him that you are *boss*. How does he expect ever to write letters to his Pa, or get to be Aide de Camp if he does not go to school and learn to write. He will go I know. He was only joking when he said he would not. I hope you will be pleasantly situated. Burlington is said to be a very nice place and nice people.[55] You will soon be more at home there than in Gravois where there is no body except your own family for whom you have much reason to care.—I hope Jennie will come on and at least spend the Winter with you. I have written to your father asking him to make his home with us. Love and kisses for you and the children. Good night.

ULYS.

City Point, Va. Sept. 30th 1864.

Dear Julia,

I have just rec'd your letter in regard to starting the children to school in Wilmington. My last letter I think entirely answers it but I write again to make sure. I would not send the children to school in Burlington. I presume there is a doubt when you will go to Phila and you want the children with you whilst I am away. If I was at home all the time it would make no diffirence,

[55]Burlington, New Jersey, near Trenton.

but housekeeping you will be lonesome with them and me both absent. We have been having great battles here such as at the begining of the War would have thrilled the whole country. Our advantages have been large and no doubt the enemy feel badly over it. One fort taken yesterday they regarded as impregnable, but our troops got over the river and surprised and drove them back so rapidly that the fort was taken almost before they were aware of it.[56] In it they had some of their finest guns, 8 in. Columbiads and Rifled guns, one of them a One hundred pounder.

I try to look at everything calmly, believe I do, therefore believe all we want to produce a speedy peace is a unity of sentiment in the North. My dispatches from Sherman shows he is doing a very greatdeel there. Gov. Brown, of Ga. (Vice President Stevens of the so called Confederacy backing him,) wants to call a session of the Legislature to take Ga. out really from the Confederacy.[57] If this is done it will be the end of rebellion, or so nearly so that the rebelling will be by one portion of the South against the other.—Love & kisses for you and the children.

ULYS.

P. S. I have a pair of very handsome pistols and the great sanitary Fair coat both of which I shall send to you by Express in a day or two. As soon as you get to housekeeping, in your own house, you had better call in all the swords, guns &c. now scattered over thc country.

[56]Union troops crossed the James River on September 29, 1864, but were unable to break through the inner defensive lines around Richmond.

[57]Sherman had spoken with two men claiming to represent Governor Joseph E. Brown (1821–1895). Despite their overtures, Brown did not attempt to arrange a separate peace.

City Point Va. Oct. 26th 1864

Dear Julia,

To-morrow a great battle will probably be fought.[58] At all events I have made all the arrangements for one and unless I conclude through the day to change my programme it will take place. I do not like to predict results therefore will say nothing about what I expect to accomplish. The cake you sent by Mr. Smith come to hand but the other you speak of having sent by Express has not. In one of your letters you ask if I accepted the house in Chicago? I did not accept or decline. I stated that I had no disposition to give up Ill. as my place of residence but the probability being that my duties hereafter would keep me most of the time in the East I had selected Phila as a place where my children could have the benefit of good schools and I could expect often to visit my family. If they were in Chicago I could not expect to see them often. I have heard nothing further since.

All are well here. Rawlins appears to have entirely recovered. Shall I have Little Rebel sent to you? If you had him you could get a little buggy and sleigh expressly for him and the children could then ride as much as they pleased. I expect when this campaign ends to send all my horses home and stay there most of the time myself when I am not visiting the different Armies. I do wish I could tell when that would be.—Love and kisses for you and the children.

ULYS.

[58]Union troops attacked east of Richmond at Darbytown Road and southwest of Petersburg at Hatcher's Run, October 27–28, 1864, but failed to gain ground.

City Point, Va Jan 1st 1865.

Dear Julia,

Happy New Year to you. Fred. starts home this morning and will tell you I am quite well. I must commence taking quinine however. Every one on the Staff have been sick, Col. Badeau and Col. Porter so much so that they had to be sent home.

I inclose you two strips of paper which I want you to read and preserve. Sherman's letter shows how noble a man he is. How few there are who when rising to popular favor as he now is would stop to say a word in defence of the only one between himself and the highest in command. I am glad to say that I appreciated Sherman from the first feeling him to be what he has proven to the world he is. Good buy.

ULYS.

Kisses for you and the children.

U.

City Point, Va, Jan. 11th 1865.

Dear Julia,

I have just rec'd a letter from Jones saying he had sent you \$475 00 This however includes the gold which I do not want you to spend. If it is necessary for you to have more money

I will try to send it. I have received a letter from Jim. Casey saying that $1400 00 back taxes are due on your fathers place and unless paid this month the place will be sold. Now I cannot afford to send $1400 there and get no return for it. I know if I pay up the taxes it will be the last I shall ever see of the money. Looking to my own interest in the matter I wrote to Ford to attend to the matter for me and to let the farm be sold for taxes and him to buy it in my name. I at the same time arranged for borrowing the money to send to him. A tax title amounts to no title atall but it is good until the money paid is refunded. If I can I will force John to make Nelly and Emma deeds to their land and probably to Fred. also.

I receive all your letters. Some of them are rather cross.— Love and kisses for you and the children.

ULYS.

By Telegraph from Hd Qurs A P Mar 30 1865

To Mrs Grant

I wrote to you today—Tell Mrs Rawlins that the Genl is not going much in the rain.

This weather is bad for us but it is Consoling to know that it rains on the enemy as well

U S GRANT
Lt Genl

Dabney's Mill Apl. 1st 1865

Dear Julia,

Another day has passed without anything decisive as to the final result so far as I have heard. This morning the enemy attacked Gn. Ord's picket line but a short distance from where I now write but got repulsed with a loss of about 60 prisoners left in our hands besides a number killed and wounded. We lost but four captured. Gn. Sheridan, far to the left, about ten miles off, has been driving the enemy all day and has killed and wounded a great number besides capturing about 200 prisoners, Since I last heard from him he has had quite a battle the result of which I have not heard.[59] I am feeling very well and full of confidence. Love and kisses for you & Jess.

ULYS,

Apl. 2d 1865

Dear Julia,

I am now writing from far inside of what was the rebel fortifications this morning but what are ours now. They are exceedingly strong and I wonder at the sucsess of our troops carrying them by storm.[60] But they did do it and without any

[59]Philip H. Sheridan (1831–1888) overran the Confederate positions at Five Forks west of Petersburg on April 1, 1865, capturing 2,500 prisoners.

[60]Grant had ordered a general assault on the Petersburg defenses at dawn on April 2, 1865. The attack broke through the Confederate lines and forced the evacuation of Petersburg and Richmond.

great loss. We have captured about 12,000 prisoners and 50 pieces of Artillery. As I write this news comes of the capture of 1000 more prisoners. Altogether this has been one of the greatest victories of the war. Greatest because it is over what the rebels have always regarded as their most invincable Army and the one used for the defince of their capitol. We may have some more hard work but I hope not.

Love and kisses for you and Jess.

ULYS.

Washington Apl. 16th 1865

Dear Julia,

I got back here about 1 p. m. yesterday and was called immediately into the presence of our new President, who had already been qualified, and the Cabinet. I telegraphed you from Baltimore and told Beckwith to do the same thing from here. You no doubt received the dispatches. All seems very quiet here. There is but little doubt but that the plot contemplated the distruction of more than the President and Sec. of State. I think now however it has expended itself and there is but little to fear. For the present I shall occupy a room in the office which is well guarded and will be occupied by Bowers and probably two or three others. I shall only go to the Hotel twice a day for my meals and will stay indoors of evenings. The change which has come upon the country so suddenly will make it necessary for me to remain in the City for several days yet. Gen. Halleck will go to Richmond to command there and Ord to Charleston.

Other changes which will have to be made, and the apparent feeling that I should remain here until everything gets into working order under the new régime will probably detain me here until next Saturday. If I can get home sooner I will do so. I hope you will be in your house in Phila when I do go home. The inconvenience of getting from the Phila depot to Burlington is about equal to the balance of the trip.

Love and kisses for you and the children.

ULYS.

Apl. 21st 1865

Dear Julia,

It is now nearly 11 O'Clock at night and I have received directions from the Sec. of War, and President, to start at once for Raleigh North Carolina.[61] I start in an hour. Gen. Meigs, Maj. Leet, Capt. Dunn, (Dunn is Capt. and Asst. Adj. Gn.) and Major Hudson go with me. I will write to you from Morehead City or New Berne.—I do hope you will have moved to Phila by the time I return. I can run up to Philadelphia easily; but to get to Burlington I have to give notice of my going to secure a train to take me the last end of the way.

I find my duties, anxieties, and the necessity for having all my wits about me, increasing instead of diminishing. I have a

[61]Sherman and Joseph E. Johnston had signed an agreement in North Carolina on April 18, 1865, that provided military and political terms for the surrender of the remaining Confederate armies. President Andrew Johnson and the cabinet rejected the agreement and ordered Grant to go to North Carolina.

Herculean task to perform and shall endeavor to do it, not to please any one, but for the interests of our great country that is now begining to loom far above all other countries, modern or ancient. What a spectacle it will be to see a country able to put down a rebellion able to put half a Million of soldiers in the field, at one time, and maintain them! That will be done and is almost done already. That Nation, united, will have a strength which will enable it to dictate to all others, *conform to justice and right*. Power I think can go no further. The moment conscience leaves, physical strength will avail nothing, in the long run.

I only sat down to write you that I was suddenly required to leave on important duty, and not feeling willing to say what that duty is, you must await my return to know more.

Love and kisses for you and the children.

U. S. GRANT

In the Field Raleigh Apl. 25th 1865

Dear Julia,

We arrived here yesterday and as I expected to return to-day did not intend to write until I returned. Now however matters have taken such a turn that I suppose Sherman will finish up matters by to-morrow night and I shall wait to see the result.[62]

[62]Grant had ordered Sherman to demand Johnston's surrender on the same terms Grant had given to Robert E. Lee at Appomattox. The new agreement was signed by Sherman and Johnston on April 26, 1865.

Raleigh is a very beautiful place. The grounds are large and filled with the most beautiful spreading oaks I ever saw. Nothing has been destroyed and the people are anxious to see peace restored so that further devastation need not take place in the country. The suffering that must exist in the South the next year, even with the war ending now, will be beyond conception. People who talk now of further retalliation and punishment, except of the political leaders, either do not conceive of the suffering endured already or they are heartless and unfeeling and wish to stay at home, out of danger, whilst the punishment is being inflicted.

Love and Kisses for you and the children,

ULYS,

CODA

Mt McGregor, Saratoga Co. N. Y.
June 29th 1885.

My Dear Wife:

There are some matters about which I would like to talk but about which I cannot. The subject would be painful to you and the children, and, by reflex, painful to me also. When I see you and them depressed I join in the feeling.

I have known for a long time that my end was approaching with certainty. How far away I could not venture to guess. I had an idea however that I would live until fall or the early part of winter. I see now, however, that the time is approaching much more rapidly. I am constantly loosing flesh and strength. The difficulty of swallowing is increasing daily. The tendency to spasms is constant. From three or four in the afternoon until relieved by Morphine I find it difficult to get breath enough to sustain me. Under these circumstances the end is not far off.

We are comparitive strangers in New York City; that is, we made it our home late in life. We have rarely if ever had serious sickness in the family, therefore have made no preparation for a place of buryal. This matter will necessarily come up at my death, and may cause you some embarassment to decide. I should myself select West Point above all other places but for the fact that in case West Point should be selected you would, when the time comes, I hope far in the future, be excluded from the same grounds. I therefore leave you free to select what you think the most appropriate place for depositing my earthly remains.

My will disposes of my property I have left with Fred. a memorandum giving some details of how the proceeds from my book are to be drawn from the publisher, and how disposed of.

Look after our dear children and direct them in the paths of rectitude. It would distress me far more to think that one of them could depart from an honorable, upright and virtuous life than it would to know they were prostrated on a bed of sickness from which they were never to arise alive. They have never given us any cause of alarm on their account. I earnestly pray they never will.

With these few injunctions, and the knowledge I have of your love and affections, and of the dutiful affection of all our children, I bid you a final farewell until we meet in another, and I trust better, world.

U. S. GRANT

P. S. This will be found in my coat after my demise.

U. S. G.

BIBLIOGRAPHICAL NOTES

SOURCES AND ACKNOWLEDGMENTS

INDEX

BIOGRAPHICAL NOTES

Julia Boggs Dent Grant was born in St. Louis County, Missouri, on January 26, 1826, the daughter of a slaveholding planter. She spent most of her childhood at White Haven, the family estate outside of St. Louis, before attending a boarding school for young women in St. Louis from 1837 to 1843. In 1844 she became engaged to Ulysses S. Grant, but because of his service in the Mexican-American War, their marriage was delayed until August 22, 1848. She accompanied Grant on postings in Detroit and Sackets Harbor, New York, 1849–52; their first son, Frederick Dent Grant, was born on May 30, 1850, and their second, Ulysses S. Grant Jr., on May 22, 1852. They were separated when Grant was posted to the Pacific coast in 1852, but reunited after he left the army in 1854 and began farming on the Dent estate. Their daughter, Ellen Wrenshall Grant, was born July 4, 1855, and their third son, Jesse Root Grant, was born February 6, 1858. The family moved to Galena, Illinois, in 1860, but was again separated by the outbreak of the Civil War; during the conflict Julia visited her husband whenever possible at his various headquarters. After the war, she enjoyed an active social life as First Lady, 1869–77, and then accompanied Grant on an around-the-world tour of Europe, the Middle East, and Asia, 1877–79. Julia helped care for Grant during his final illness and was present at his death; she later received over $400,000 in royalties from sales of *Personal Memoirs of*

U. S. Grant. In the late 1880s she began dictating her own memoirs, but was unable to make a satisfactory arrangement for their publication; they were published posthumously in 1975 as *The Personal Memoirs of Julia Dent Grant*, edited by John Y. Simon. During the 1890s she regularly visited California, where many of her children and grandchildren lived. She died in Washington, D.C., from heart and kidney failure on December 14, 1902.

Ulysses S. Grant was born in Point Pleasant, Ohio, on April 22, 1822, the son of a tanner. He graduated from West Point in 1843 and was commissioned in the 4th Infantry Regiment. The next year he became engaged to Julia Boggs Dent. Grant served in the Mexican-American War, 1846–48, fighting in several battles. In 1848 he married Julia Dent; they had four children. Grant resigned his commission after being promoted to captain in 1854. Over the next four years he cleared and farmed land on the Dent estate outside St. Louis and sold firewood in the city. From 1858 to 1860 Grant worked as a real estate agent and clerk in St. Louis before moving to Galena, Illinois, where he helped his brothers run a leather goods store. Following the outbreak of the Civil War, Grant was commissioned as colonel of the 21st Illinois Volunteers in June 1861. He was promoted to brigadier general, August 1861, and to major general of volunteers, February 1862, after his victories at Forts Henry and Donelson. Grant defeated the Confederates at Shiloh, April 1862, captured Vicksburg, Mississippi, July 1863, and won the battle of Chattanooga, November 1863. He was promoted to lieutenant general and named general-in-chief of the Union armies in March 1864. After naming William T. Sherman as his successor in command of the western theater, Grant accompanied the Army of the Potomac during the campaign in Virginia, May–June 1864, and the siege of Petersburg,

June 1864–April 1865, before accepting the surrender of Robert E. Lee at Appomattox Court House, April 9, 1865. Promoted to general, July 1866, he served as secretary of war ad interim, August 1867–January 1868. Nominated for president by the Republican Party in 1868, Grant defeated Democrat Horatio Seymour, won reelection in 1872 by defeating Liberal Republican Horace Greeley, and served as President of the United States, 1869–77. After leaving the White House the former president toured Europe, the Middle East, and Asia, 1877–79. An attempt by his supporters to nominate him for a third term at the Republican convention in 1880 failed. Grant worked on Wall Street, 1881–84, and was financially ruined when the private banking firm of Grant & Ward collapsed. He wrote *Personal Memoirs of U. S. Grant*, 1884–85, while suffering from throat cancer, and completed the manuscript days before his death at Mount McGregor, New York, on July 23, 1885.

SOURCES AND ACKNOWLEDGMENTS

The texts of the eighty-five letters included in this book are taken from *The Papers of Ulysses S. Grant*, edited by John Y. Simon and John F. Marszalek (32 volumes to date, Carbondale: Southern Illinois University Press, 1967–2012). Volume 1 (1967), Volume 2 (1969), Volume 4 (1972), Volume 5 (1973), Volume 7 (1979), Volume 8 (1979), Volume 9 (1982), Volume 10 (1982), Volume 11 (1984), Volume 12 (1985), Volume 13 (1985), Volume 14 (1985), Volume 31 (2009), edited by John Y. Simon. Copyright © 1967, 1969, 1972, 1973, 1979, 1982, 1984, 1985, 2009 by the Ulysses S. Grant Association. Reprinted with the permission of The Ulysses S. Grant Association.

Three asterisks *** are used in this book to indicate where Julia Dent Grant crossed out words in the manuscript of a letter, while a bracketed space [ ] is used to indicate where words are missing or illegible as a result of damage to the manuscript of a letter. The texts of the letters chosen for inclusion here are printed without change, except for the correction of typographical errors and slips of the pen. Spelling, punctuation, and capitalization are often expressive features and are not altered, even when inconsistent or irregular.

INDEX

☆ ☆ ☆